"Christine Valters Paintner invites ι﹍﹍﹍﹍﹍﹍ way of being and teaches us how to live *from* there. Warm-hearted, its wisdom keeps us company whether we are in grief's wilderness, a joyful time, or another liminal place. Making space for our true, loving self to awaken and reawaken, it shares ways to travel soulcraft's healing path together and walks us home."

Carmen Acevedo Butcher
Poet and translator of *The Cloud of Unknowing* and *Practice of the Presence*

"Reading a book by Christine Valters Paintner is like going on a retreat in your own home. She tells meaningful stories, offers insightful guidance, and presents practical ways to bring spirituality into your heart, body, and soul. With *The Love of Thousands*, she invites readers into one of the most beautiful elements of Christian spirituality: the Communion of Saints (and angels and ancestors). But this is no mere abstract doctrine—the wisdom offered here can help make the love of our heavenly companions truly an embodied presence in our lives."

Carl McColman
Author of *The New Big Book of Christian Mysticism*

"Reading *The Love of Thousands* is like gathering around a campfire on a clear starlit night or plunging into a cold refreshing stream. It awakens what we know by heart, lifting up simple practices that help us cultivate mystical presence. Drawing deeply from the well of human experience, Christine Valters Paintner once again gives us a reliable hope, not just for our individual lives but for the collective wounds plaguing our planet."

Dori Grinenko Baker
Coauthor of *Another Way*

"With her trademark commingling of erudite research and compassionate intimacy, Christine Valters Paintner gently pulls back the veils of both time and space that we might see all those who have come before us looking lovingly upon us in the shadow of every tree, in the echo of every bird's song. Contemplative prayers and practices invite us into a sacred experience of the love that came before us, the love that surrounds us still, guiding us into the profound peace of knowing that we never walk alone."

Cameron Bellm
Catholic author and speaker

"If Christine Valters Paintner simply took us on a journey in her book, *The Love of Thousands*, that would be enough. In this magical and mystical work, which contains the quotes from a fantastic array of sages, she also opens the space for us to robustly experience our own spiritual pilgrimage as well. Her book is actually a retreat on knowing life more richly by revisiting such experiences as impermanence and vulnerability. By drawing from a breadth of spiritual traditions and personal insights, she also helps us understand time and attention not as mere concepts, but as lenses that need to be polished and intently looked through differently, honestly, hopefully. In encountering her words, I felt as if Paintner was sitting alongside me and encouraging me to breathe in life and become open to relics, sainthood, ancestry, meditation, angelic relationships, and feast days in ways that those whom I have admired did long before me. She constantly challenged me to calmly and humbly open myself to being on the edge of wonder and awe, to appreciate life's 'thin places,' even when what I first encountered was, to my mind, darkness. My hope is that the new consciousness and meditative way of life that this spurred on in me will have a similar impact on you as well."

Robert J. Wicks
Author of *Riding the Dragon*

THE LOVE OF THOUSANDS

HOW ANGELS, SAINTS, AND ANCESTORS
WALK WITH US TOWARD HOLINESS

CHRISTINE VALTERS PAINTNER

SORIN BOOKS  Notre Dame, IN

http://www.avemariapress.com/sorin-books

Paperback: ISBN-13 978-1-932057-33-1

E-book: ISBN-13 978-1-932057-34-8

Cover image "Communion of Saints" © 2023 Elise Ritter, elise-ritter.pixels.com, @eliseritterartist.

Cover and text design by Samantha Watson.

Printed and bound in the United States of America.

Library of Congress Cataloging-in-Publication Data is available.

Walking, I can almost hear the redwoods beating. And the oceans are above me here, rolling clouds, heavy and dark. It is winter and there is smoke from the fires. It is a world of elemental attention, of all things working together, listening to what speaks in the blood. Whichever road I follow, I walk in the land of many gods, and they love and eat one another. Suddenly all my ancestors are behind me. Be still, they say. Watch and listen. You are the result of the love of thousands.

—Linda Hogan, *Dwellings: A Spiritual History of the Living World*

To my wise and well ancestors,
spanning New England, England,
Latvia, Austria, Slovenia, Hungary,
and the Czech Republic,
who shower me with love and support
and cheer me on daily:
all I do is because of your courage and inspiration.

CONTENTS

INTRODUCTION

What is the knocking?
What is the knocking at the door in the night?
It is somebody wants to do us harm.
No, no, it is the three strange angels.
Admit them, admit them.

—D. H. Lawrence, excerpt from
"Song of a Man Who Has Come Through"

The quote by Chickasaw poet and writer Linda Hogan I share as an epigraph to this book is one that has guided my journey more deeply into the world of angels, saints, and ancestors for many years.

At its foundation, it is a journey of opening our hearts to the love of all those sacred beings who dwell in spiritual form across the veil. Our Western minds may tell us that what we see is all there is, but the religious and mystical imagination knows a deeper truth.

Various religious traditions have taught about the existence of angels, saints, and ancestors for millennia. The God I believe in is a God of Love, a divine being from whom all of creation erupted out of this foundation of Love.

In a world so filled with struggles, discord, and violence, I know I need as many reminders of the Love that undergirds and infuses all of life. Those beings who dwell in the light of the Divine Presence extend themselves toward us in loving care and compassion. They are resources to help sustain and inspire us. All we need to do is look with eyes of the heart. All we need to do is open ourselves to an encounter.

THRESHOLDS AND THE OTHERWORLD

Thresholds are potent doorways between the old and the new. When we step onto a threshold in our lives, we release an old identity or old patterns and await the new birthing. It can be uncomfortable at times to rest in this space of waiting, of not knowing what things will look like. But we can cultivate our capacity to breathe deeply and stay present to what is unfolding within us through retreat time.

To connect with the Otherworld—the world beyond the veil of appearances—means developing our intuitive skills and vision. It means trusting the messages from our heart and gut, rather than only what the mind shows us and our culture tells us is valuable. It means listening to daydreams and night dreams and paying attention to synchronicities— when a symbol or image starts to show up in multiple ways and places. It means spending time in the natural world and letting feather, fur, and fin reveal dimensions of our longing to us. It means listening for leaf erupting from branch and blossom emerging from stem without trying to figure things out. It means cultivating the capacity to let things be organic and emerge slowly.

For some it might mean suspending disbelief in the possibility of this kind of love and connection long enough for messages to be revealed. As Mark's gospel tells us, "The Spirit drove [Jesus] out into the desert, and he remained in the desert for forty days, tempted by Satan. He was among wild beasts, and the angels ministered to him" (1:12–13, NABRE). And this version from *The Message* by Eugene Peterson: "At once, this same Spirit pushed Jesus out into the wild. For forty wilderness days and nights he was tested by Satan. Wild animals were his companions, and angels took care of him."

This is our starting place: going out into the wilderness of our lives, the threshold space where we release the old and anticipate the new, and in this liminal place we know that angels and other spiritual beings surround us and attend to us.

JOURNEY OF WRITING THIS BOOK

In many ways I have been working on the materials in this book for almost twenty years. Or perhaps it is more accurate to say the subject matter has been working on me. The journey began in earnest two years after my mother died and I walked into the office of a Jungian analyst who is still my spiritual director all these years later. He introduced me to the concept of family systems theory and psychologist Carl Jung's teachings about the wounds of our ancestors, which sparked many healing journeys.

During this season of grief, I also began to call on the angels and saints much more urgently than I had before to support me in my journey of loss. The story of Jacob wrestling with the angel, which I will explore in a later chapter, felt like an emblem of my own grappling with who God was for me in the wake of such loss.

I knew St. Benedict could help steady me and keep me grounded in my contemplative practice. St. Francis could invite me to befriend Death as a Sister. St. Hildegard could offer me her healing balms and elixirs through a reminder of God's greening power flowing freely. The archangels offered their protection, healing, and guidance through that difficult terrain.

Over the years, the angels, saints, and mystics have been at the heart of much of my teaching and retreat work. Many pilgrims and seekers joined me who already had a connection to these presences, and many came who longed for some kind of relationship but didn't have the language or experience to understand how that might be possible. My students and retreat participants have always been wise teachers for me, with questions that gently probe me deeper and their own wisdom and insights that inspire me to continue.

OVERVIEW OF THIS BOOK

This book began in my mind as a book about relating to ancestors. My own ancestral healing journey has been such a significant part of my spiritual path that I wanted to invite others into that work.

As I developed the work, I realized that while many of us are drawn to ancestral work because of the generational wounds we are aware need healing, there is also a wide communion of what we might call the "wise and well ancestors." These are the ones who embody wholeness and love in their fullness already and can offer us blessings. They can help us to heal the parts of our family lines that need tending.

The Catholic Church teaches that there are officially canonized saints who have gone through a formal process of being recognized as having value for the whole community. But they also recognize the wider "Communion of Saints" who have passed over and are fully wise, well, and ready to offer us in this earthly realm guidance and care. I realized the saints and ancestors are part of one wider circle of care that surrounds us.

Then came the angels, who I have always been drawn to in cemeteries, especially the large stone statues. For me, these statues symbolize their weight and density, albeit in spiritual form. As I started to expand my own awareness of the invisible world and cultivate a relationship with angels, I was delighted to discover these beings are recognized and honored not just in Christianity but also in Judaism and Islam. Somehow the way they have inspired so many faithful opened my heart to a deeper relationship with the ways they are present to us.

The book begins with three chapters on the angels, starting with exploring the four archangels, then understanding guardian angels, and finally wrestling with angels. Not all encounters with angels feel full of ease and clarity, and I want to honor that experience.

The next three chapters explore the saints and mystics, those who cultivated an expansive heart and vision of the Divine present everywhere. First, I explore how we are all called to this pathway of being mystics and saints. Then I explore the tradition of relics and how a connection to the physical remains of the saints helps us to celebrate the

Incarnation and a faith that is deeply embodied. And finally, I consider the practice of pilgrimage, which has gained such popularity over recent years, as a way to connect with the saints through landscape.

Finally, in the section on ancestors, I invite us first to claim the blessings the wise and well ones have for us and then to explore the journey of healing the wounds of our lineages, embrace grief, and find ways to connect more deeply with the ancestors through pilgrimage, stories, song, language, and food traditions. It closes with chapters on becoming wise and well ancestors ourselves and connecting to Earth as an ancestor.

The conclusion brings these threads together, weaving the love of thousands into a vision of support for our growing wholeness. While many of the ideas I draw from here are rooted in Catholic theological tradition, my hope is that this book will open up the experience of angels, saints, and ancestors to anyone, regardless of institutional affiliation.

Structure of the Chapters

Each chapter begins with a reflection on the theme to invite you into a deeper relationship with the angels, saints, or ancestors. These are followed by a suggestion for a specific practice or way of being you can cultivate to embody this theme. Then I offer a meditation to move the contemplation from your head into your heart space. Each chapter includes a suggestion for a creative exploration, such as creating altars for the invisible realm and various writing explorations to help you break open the material in a creative way. The creative practices are always meant as journeys of discovery rather than the pursuit of perfection. Let yourself get messy; enjoy the process. Finally, the chapters each close with a unique blessing for the work you've been doing as you traverse the pages.

How to Use This Book

As with most of the books I write, my suggestion is to move through the chapters slowly, making time to read, reflect, practice, contemplate, and create so that integration might have room to take root. You could do this over a series of fourteen weeks or even the span of a year, taking a chapter per week or one or two per month. You might consider inviting a group of other pilgrims together to gather regularly and share what you are discovering as you move through the materials.

Disclaimer

In this book I mention several people whose work has been influential to my development and the formulation of this book. However, the mention of their books and their work is not an endorsement of all of their work or of their personal lives. The spiritual guides whom I find helpful will not always be the ones who resonate with your journey. All our journeys will be different, and you will discern your own spiritual guides in addition to, or instead of, mine. Please do your own due diligence when considering what books and authors to explore next in your own journey.

Now, let's begin.

Part One

ANGELS

1

CALLING ON THE
ARCHANGELS

Angels are central to that same history of yearning
and the search to connect the visible with invisible. In
cultures stretching back tens of thousands of years,
there have been winged creatures who serve the gods
and who make a bridge, or ladder, between the divine
realm and the earthly one.

—Peter Stanford, *Angels: A History*

Angels appear throughout the Hebrew and Christian scriptures as well
as in the Qur'an. All three Abrahamic traditions affirm the existence
of these invisible beings who serve as protectors, messengers, healers,
and bearers of wisdom.

According to the Talmud, the essence of angels is fire. Psalm 104
tells us God makes "the winds [his] messengers, fire and flame [his]
ministers" (v. 4). Angels are made of fire and sustained by fire. In Islam
angels are made from light itself; they are light beings. Many Christians
would ask what angels were made of. Light was St. Augustine's clear

response, emphasizing what we learn from both Hebrew and Islamic sources. Augustine, in the *City of God*, suggests that angels were created right at the start of the whole process of creation. When God proclaims "Let there be light" (Gn 1:3), the sun, moon, and stars were called into existence, but the angels were as well. "As intermediaries," Augustine proposed, "angels' entire being was so designed as to allow God's light to shine through them into humanity."[1] Angels were translucent windows onto the sacred luminosity shimmering in the world.

In the Celtic tradition in Ireland, the Otherworld is the dwelling place of gods, other supernatural beings, and ancestors. It is an elusive place of beauty and abundance as well as a threshold place. There is no direct portal to it, but there are moments when the doorway appears, and we are able to experience a connection to the sacred in a more concrete way than in ordinary time. There are openings that break through our everyday vision so we can see angels at work in the world.

As author Peter Stanford writes in the opening quote of this chapter, angels create bridges and ladders between the heavenly and earthly worlds. We might think of the story of Jacob's dream of a ladder in Genesis 28:11–12: "He came to a certain place and stayed there for the night, because the sun had set. Taking one of the stones of the place, he put it under his head and lay down in that place. And he dreamed that there was a ladder set up on the earth, the top of it reaching to heaven; and the angels of God were ascending and descending on it."

God then appears in the dream and promises Jacob many descendants and that God will abide with him. When Jacob awakens from his dream he says, "Surely the LORD is in this place—and I did not know it!" (Gn 28:16). And goes on to say, "How awesome is this place! This is none other than the house of God, and this is the gate of heaven" (Gn 28:17).

In the dream, angels are ascending and descending the ladder that connects the Divine and human. Jacob's dream reveals the place where he slept as the very gate of heaven, a doorway or threshold place that reflects this human desire to connect with the invisible realms and the beings who dwell there. From Jacob to us, we all have a longing to reach into the invisible world and receive its wisdom for comfort and courage.

After noting how angels create bridges and ladders between us and the heavenly realms, Stanford goes on to write, "Yet angels have been, for millennia, in scriptures and myths, hearts and minds, an expression of human aspiration, hope and expectation, an in-built instinct to engage not only with invisible worlds, but with invisible beings too, as a way of relieving anxiety about living, and about the inevitability of death."[2] Angels point to a very real human longing to have a connection to something larger than us to guide and protect us. Having a way to connect with these celestial messengers and guides through the ladders they create is a way to reassure ourselves that we have not been left alone in this world. The wisdom traditions make this clear: there is a multitude of presences, and the love of thousands is available to us. We just have to seek that love through the connections they've made for us.

The Archangels

In the Christian scriptures we are presented with three of the four archangels: Michael, Gabriel, and Raphael. Uriel, the fourth, is named in other sources. These four archangels are also named in Jewish texts and prayers.

Archangel Michael: Warrior

The earliest surviving mentions of Michael's name are in the Jewish book of Enoch, written in the second century BCE, where he is listed as one of seven archangels (the others are named there as Raphael, Gabriel, Uriel, Sariel, Raguel, and Remiel). There he is noted as the chief of the angels and archangels and as responsible for the care of Israel. Christianity embraced many of the Jewish traditions concerning Michael, and he is mentioned explicitly in Revelation 12:7–12, where he does battle with Satan, casting him out of heaven. Because of this battle with Satan, Michael is often depicted wielding a sword and defeating a dragon. He is also mentioned in the Qur'an.

In the book of Tobit, a slightly later Jewish work, the archangels are said to "stand ready and enter before the glory of the Lord" (12:15). We can presume that because the archangels are mentioned without further explanation in this book, the community was already familiar with them. Michael is mentioned again in the last chapters of the book of Daniel, a book about an apocalypse, where it is said, "Michael, the great prince, the protector of your people, shall arise" (12:1).

In the Eastern Orthodox tradition, there is also a devotion to the archangels, as well as guardian angels.[3] Archangel Michael appears in many of the icons in Orthodox churches and is mentioned in many of their hymns and prayers. Michael is generally viewed as the angelic warrior who does battle with the inner and outer presence of evil in the world. He is also depicted at times as being the angel of death, offering each soul a chance at redemption and carrying the souls of the dead to heaven.

St. Francis had a special devotion to the archangel Michael, especially in his role as the one who would transport the dead, using his strong, protective wings to carry souls from their earthly bodies to heaven, where their eternal fate would be determined. Life was felt to be very fragile during St. Francis's time, and the fate of one's soul was an intimate and pressing concern.

Because of Michael's ascent toward the sky, those who had lost a loved one would often climb to the peak of a mountain to offer their prayers to Michael to usher their beloved ones into Paradise, in the hope that from the height their prayers would reach him more directly.[4]

Michael has been present across time and traditions as a fierce protective presence who also stands at the threshold between life and death. He is the archetype of the sacred warrior, defending life and virtue.

Archangel Gabriel: Messenger

Gabriel also appears in the book of Enoch, among other ancient Jewish texts. Along with Michael, Gabriel is described as the guardian angel of Israel. He also appears as a celestial messenger in the book of Daniel, interpreting and explaining Daniel's visions. In Islam, Gabriel is the archangel sent by God to Muhammed and is believed to have revealed the first verses of the Qur'an.

You are likely most familiar with Gabriel from his appearances in the Christian scriptures. He appears in Luke's gospel to announce the births of John the Baptist to Zechariah and of Jesus to Mary in the Annunciation: "He is the herald, the one who announces good news and reveals the hidden plans of God."[5] Gabriel is the archetypal messenger, bringing important questions and invitations to humans.

In art, Gabriel is often depicted wearing blue or white garments while carrying a lily, a trumpet, a lantern, a scroll, a scepter, or a branch from paradise. He is a symbol for all the ways we receive calls or invitations in our lives that feel as if they are from a higher source.

Archangel Raphael: Healer

The name *Raphael* means "God has healed" in Hebrew. He is mentioned in the Hebrew scriptures in the books of Enoch and Tobit. In Tobit he acts as physician to expel demons and heal Tobit's eyes. In Enoch he is set over all disease and the wounds of the children. He later became identified in Jewish tradition as one of the three celestial visitors whom Abraham entertained in the oak grove of Mamre (see Genesis 18:1–14). Michael, as the greatest, walks in the middle, with Gabriel to his left and Raphael to his right.

Raphael is not named in the Christian scriptures or the Qur'an, but he later becomes identified with healing. He is connected to the unnamed angel who stirs the waters at the Pool of Bethesda in John's gospel.

Raphael is believed to help protect pilgrims on their journeys and is sometimes depicted as holding a staff. He is the archetype of the one who brings physical and spiritual wholeness.

Archangel Uriel: Wisdom-Bearer

The name *Uriel* means "light of God" in Hebrew; it is the name of one of the archangels who is mentioned in the post-Exilic rabbinic tradition and in certain Christian traditions. He is well known in the Russian Orthodox tradition and in the Anglican Church. Uriel is also known as a keeper of knowledge and archangel of wisdom. He is generally not depicted in art as frequently as the others, but when he does appear, he sometimes holds a light in his open palm to symbolize truth.

Uriel is generally the fourth archangel added to the original named three (Michael, Gabriel, and Raphael) to represent the four cardinal points of north, east, south, and west. As we will see at the end of this chapter, there is a traditional Jewish prayer recited at bedtime that places the four archangels around us, to the right, to the left, before, and behind.

THE PRESENCE OF THE ARCHANGELS

In early December 2010 I was heading from Seattle, Washington, where I lived at the time, to Vienna, Austria, for a time of retreat and writing. Vienna is where my father grew up and is now buried alongside his parents and is a place of renewal for me. It had been an especially hard autumn with our beloved dog dying of dementia and my dear mother-in-law's own Alzheimer's progressing at such a rapid rate she no longer recognized loved ones. I was traveling by myself, and my husband, John, was going to meet me a couple of weeks later so we could celebrate a quiet Christmas together.

The day after I arrived in Vienna, I began having leg pain, but I thought it was because of the long flights, that I just needed to stretch and walk it off. Three days later, I started feeling shortness of breath while wandering all over that city I love so much. Finally, the fourth day after arriving, I woke up to pain and swelling in my leg and realized that I likely had a blood clot.

I went to the emergency room and was told to sit in a wheelchair and not move at all because, if I did move and did have a blood clot, the clot could dislodge and kill me instantly. I waited for several hours, having an ultrasound and a CT scan that showed deep vein thrombosis and a pulmonary embolism. I spent the next few nights in the hospital as they administered blood thinners, and I began to recover. The doctor told me one in three people with pulmonary embolisms die, so I was quite lucky given I was traipsing all over the city on foot.

I felt death had come very close to me and a fierceness in me had clung to life. Even more than that, I felt a powerful presence, a strength I was not familiar with.

John rescheduled his flight to arrive early and be with me. After being released from the hospital, we wandered slowly together over cobblestone streets, grateful to be alive and together. We passed by St. Michael's Church across from the Imperial Palace. I know this church well, but this time I saw the stone statue of Michael on the roof of the portico in a new way. His strong body lifted a sword above his head, wings spread behind him. He was suspended in a moment of fierce protection. In that moment, I felt a knowing, a sense of connection I hadn't felt before, as though my body knew that Michael, at least as an archetypal energy, had come to visit me, to perhaps defeat death until a later time.

Perhaps the archangels come to visit each of us when we need them most, even if we don't recognize them in the moment. Consider the times in your life when you were given protection from danger, a powerful message, a potent healing, or a profound sense of wisdom, and see if you can imagine one of them shimmering there beneath the surface of your experience.

PRACTICE
Becoming Fully Present

One of the core assumptions of this book is that not only are there thousands of spiritual beings (angels, saints, and ancestors) who dwell just across the veil between worlds but also that they desire to be in relationship with us. Contemplate for a moment the love of thousands awaiting you to turn toward them, to be present with them, to receive their wisdom, and to know yourself as deeply loved.

We might consider the ways we cultivate relationships in the human realm: by giving our full attention to a loved one's needs and desires, committing regular time to nurturing this connection by making it a priority in our lives, letting mutuality flourish, and growing in trust of their intentions and dreams. How often are we with a friend or spouse, and we miss what they are saying to us because we are distracted by our own thoughts, by technology, or by fatigue or worry? We only deepen into our intimate connections when we bring ourselves present to our time spent with loved ones. When we bring our full attention, commit our time and presence, honor mutuality, and nourish trust, our friendships flourish. I think of the heartfelt conversations I have with dear soul friends, people who know my vulnerabilities and cherish me. Conversation is often sacramental, because speaking our stories and being heard, witnessing others into speech, are graced moments when we often experience moments of transformation.

These ways of being with our human companions—attention, time, mutuality, trust, and vulnerability—are equally important practices to consider when encouraging connection with the spiritual beings who long to support us and communicate with us.

The first two aspects—time and attention—mean that we intentionally set aside moments of the day to bring our full presence to the angels (and later in this book, to the saints and ancestors). We can begin to integrate this into our morning and evening prayer times, simply listening for what they might have to say to us or remembering when they appeared in some form to support us. Was there a moment we felt love reaching toward us from beyond the veil? When we had a sense of a comforting, loving presence with us amid the daily struggles of our lives?

Mutuality means learning to lean into their wisdom for us and seeing angels as partners in the journey of spiritual transformation. We allow them their full agency as they allow ours. Over time, as we begin to see patterns of support emerge in our days and feel their presence in our prayer moments, trust is fostered. We begin to trust our own experience and intuition that angels are real and available to us. And we trust the reality of them in our lives.

From this space of nurtured time and attention, of mutuality and trust, we learn to offer our vulnerability to the angels. We sense their deep care for us in moments of tenderness and uncertainty. We may find ourselves able to consciously name those moments of disorientation and unknowing and reaching out for help that had previously been unconscious.

The most important step to deepening our relationship with the archangels is to make the commitment to be available for this relationship, to practice presence. The more we show up, the more we can deepen our connection to the angels and know their love and care for our lives. The more we weave an awareness of the angels into our prayers, the more they become real to us.

Jewish Bedtime Shema Liturgy

In the Jewish tradition, part of the Shema liturgy at bedtime is to call on the presence of the archangels to guard over us at night. We will be working with this prayer in the guided meditation later in this chapter. This translation is from Rabbi Rachel Barenblat:

> In the name of God, the God of Israel
> On my right is Michael, on my left is Gavriel
> In front of me is Uriel, behind me Raphael
> And all above, surrounding me, Shechinat-El.[6]

When we go to sleep, we surrender our burdens and ask God to carry them. We have to trust that things will continue on without our work and worry. Asking the archangels to surround us is another guard against anxiety and an invitation to solace. When we rise, we offer gratitude for the gift of another day.

The idea that the archangels govern Earth's four cardinal points comes from various Hebrew and Christian passages in which God mentions the four winds of heaven. Some of these passages are as follows:

> Flee from the land of the north, says the LORD; for I have spread you abroad like the four winds of heaven, says the LORD. (Zec 2:6)

> I, Daniel, saw in my vision by night the four winds of heaven stirring up the great sea. (Dn 7:2)

> And he will send out his angels with a loud trumpet call, and
> they will gather his elect from the four winds, from one end
> of heaven to the other. (Mt 24:31)

We find this idea of calling in the presence of the sacred in the four directions in the Celtic practice of encircling prayer, such as when St. Patrick invokes Christ behind, before, to our right, and to our left.

MEDITATION
Calling the Four Archangels

Consider engaging in this meditation at bedtime while lying down and preparing for sleep.[7]

Take several slow, deep breaths. With each exhale imagine that you are releasing the tensions and stresses of the day. See yourself intentionally letting go of whatever you are carrying and placing it in the arms of the Beloved to hold for you.

Drop your awareness to your heart center. Call on the Divine Presence with whatever name you choose. Ask the Source of Life to carry your burdens and worries as you go to sleep and to strengthen you through the presence of the archangels.

Call upon the archangel Michael to stand on your right side. Michael is the warrior and defender of boundaries. Ask Michael to be with you through the night, warding off anything that does not contribute to your rest and well-being. Imagine yourself leaning toward the right into Michael's strength, and notice the quality of light he brings.

Call upon the archangel Gabriel to stand on your left side. Gabriel is the messenger, the one who summons you to your holy call in life. Ask Gabriel to be with you through the night, making space in your heart for the creative birthings God desires to cocreate with you. Ask that he show up in your dreams and intuitions upon awakening. Imagine yourself leaning toward the left into Gabriel's presence, and notice the quality of light he brings.

Call upon the archangel Uriel to be in front of you. Uriel is the bearer of wisdom and insight. Ask Uriel to be with you, revealing new wisdom to your heart so that you might gain clarity about your place in the world. Imagine yourself leaning forward slightly into Uriel's strength, and notice the quality of light he brings.

Call upon the archangel Raphael to stand behind you. Raphael is the healer who helps to remind you of your wholeness and repairs any places of brokenness within your body and soul. Imagine yourself leaning back into Raphael's embrace, and notice the quality of light he brings.

Call upon the Divine in her feminine presence as Shechinah, which in Hebrew means "God's dwelling place" and is a feminine noun, or as Sophia, one of the Christian names for Holy Wisdom. Ask that she draw together the light from each of the archangels into one radiant embrace. If there is anything remaining that you are holding onto as you prepare for night's gift of darkness, rest, and mystery, see if you can surrender it over to her loving arms. Rest here a while, and let yourself drift into sleep.

CREATIVE EXPLORATION
Creating an Archangel Altar

Creating an altar is a simple and profound way to cultivate and nurture an ongoing relationship with the unseen world. Altars are ancient practices that serve as meeting points between heaven and earth. They are thresholds that spark our vision of what was formerly invisible to us. We choose items to include on the altar because of how they point us to a deeper awareness of the invisible presence of sacred beings.

Over the course of this book I will invite you to create an altar for the angels, one for the saints, and one for the ancestors. This could easily be one larger altar that honors all three of these categories of beings and spirits, or it could be three smaller altars spread throughout your home.

I suggest you keep your archangel altar quite simple. An easy way to go about this is to place a candle in the center of your altar space and then find four symbols, one for each of the associations with the archangels. See how you might express the quality of protection, being a messenger, healing, and wisdom. On my own altar I include a small branch with a thorn to evoke the sense of boundaries, a feather to represent a quill for communication, a vial of oil as a healing balm, and a small wooden heart as a reminder that wisdom dwells within. You might go for a contemplative walk and see what symbols nature offers up when you bring your desire and intention out into the world of creation. You can orient the symbols in the four directions as well to invoke that sense of the archangels' presence surrounding you.

Let your altar come together over a few days or even weeks as needed. Let part of your prayer be to ask for guidance for the perfect symbols for you to express your connection to these qualities the archangels bring into your life.

Feast Days

Another way to cultivate your relationship with angels is by marking your calendar with their feast days, similar to how you would mark down the birthday of a loved one.

I include the Roman Catholic feast days for each of the archangels below as well as the Feast of the Archangels and the Feast of the Guardian Angels. These do sometimes vary across denominations and traditions. It should also be noted that in 1969, the Catholic Church transferred the feasts of Gabriel and Raphael to the Feast of Michael to be celebrated altogether as the Feast of the Archangels. I like noting them separately as well as together, so you can choose which you prefer. There is always a reason to celebrate.

Feast of St. Michael: September 29
Feast of St. Gabriel: March 24 (day before Feast of the Annunciation)
Feast of St. Raphael: October 24
Feast of St. Uriel: November 8
Feast of the Archangels: September 29
Feast of the Guardian Angels: October 2

In Eastern Orthodox churches, every Monday throughout the year is dedicated to the angels. Partaking in that practice is another way to honor and remember them if so desired.

Blessing of the Archangels

This blessing rises on the wings of the archangels.
In moments of vulnerability,
may Michael protect you from harm.
Feel his wings surround you,
shielding you from arrows of doubt, despair,
ill will and manipulation.
May he help you to know your own strength
emerging from within like a storm
gathering force, a fierceness to shelter
what and whom you love most.
When you cross that final luminous threshold
into the next life,
may Michael companion you
and bring you courage to open your eyes
and heart wide, to step into a new adventure.
In moments of discernment,
may you listen for Gabriel's call,
appearing as he did to Zechariah and Mary.
Receive him as divine messenger
and summon your courage
to offer your heartfelt yes
to this holy birthing.
When visions come in night dreams
and day-wondering, call on Gabriel
to help you listen for the meaning,
to unlock symbols like an ancient map
pointing the way ahead.
In moments of wounding and illness,
may you experience the healing force of Raphael

who stirred the waters at the Pool of Bethesda,
restoring all to wholeness again.
Call on him to help knit together every rupture,
to return every ache to aliveness,
every disease to vibrancy.
And in the absence of cure,
may Raphael bring the gentle healing
of spirit, a heart expanded,
an embrace of tears and laughter.
In moments of confusion
and seasons of change,
may you embrace the wisdom of Uriel
named the Light-Bringer
guiding you along the path.
Wisdom comes from lived experience,
a deep inner knowing of life's meaning
wrought from struggle and challenge.
Let Uriel help you stay present
in the midst of a difficult season,
help you to see the grace at work
amidst the sorrow and loss.
May he bring clarity and a renewed heart.
May the archangels surround you,
uplift you, guide you, and heal you.
May you know their luminous presence
at every season of your life.

2

ENCOUNTERING YOUR GUARDIAN ANGEL

With all my heart
    I praise you, LORD.
In the presence of angels
    I sing your praises.
I worship at your holy temple
and praise you for your love
    and your faithfulness.

—Psalm 138:1–2a (Contemporary English Version)

My heart sank when I stepped tentatively into my mother's hospital room. She lay in bed connected to a complex web of tubes and wires, eyes shut. The thin skin on her face was sunken and bruised; her lips were raw. She had serious pneumonia that had entered her bloodstream, causing septicemia that led to unconsciousness, kidney failure, an inability to breathe without a respirator, and dangerously low blood pressure. The previous evening, she had gone into cardiac arrest twice, but the hospital staff had resuscitated her.

This wasn't supposed to happen. She had just spent twelve weeks in this same hospital recovering from a bone infection, and all she longed for during that time was to go home. She had only been home for a week; now she was back in the same hospital, and my heart was breaking. I had received a call from the hospital telling me of her condition in the morning; I was on a plane within a couple of hours from my home in Seattle to her home in Sacramento, where I picked up a car at the airport and drove straight to see her.

I took a deep breath and began to pray those feverish prayers of desperation as death whispered in my ear, those prayers when you hope the way you have lived your life somehow earns the right to a miracle even though you are not sure you believe in miracles and deep down you know that's not how the world works. I prayed that she would be able to go home. But as day gave way to night, I realized that the meaning of that prayer had shifted. Going home would most likely mean something entirely different this time.

The next day my husband, John, arrived from Seattle, and the day after that my mother's sister and her husband flew out from Maine. I spent the hours before and after they arrived perched on the edge of my mother's bed, rubbing hospital lotion on her arms and legs as a private act of anointing. Each stroke became its own kind of blessing.

"She can hear you," the nurses kept assuring me, despite her not being conscious, and so I sang simple chants to her that were choked by my tears. Words of longing would rise up in me, and I would bathe her in song. I told her again and again that I loved her, that she was beautiful, and that I wanted more than anything for her to open her eyes again and gaze on me. Even in those moments, as she pressed against life's edges, she was as beautiful as she had ever been.

After two days spent with her, bathed in the harsh green glow of fluorescent hospital lights, the reality of her condition slowly knit itself into my bones with an ache unlike any I had ever felt. I told the doctor to take my mother off of life support. I was an only child, and my father had died seven years prior, so the decision was left to me. My family supported me through it, but there was a silent assent that, informed by doctors, this would ultimately be my choice to make. The nurse had told me the doctor might resist, that he didn't like giving up without a long fight, but instead he simply agreed and said I had made a wise choice.

They left the respirator on so she wouldn't suffocate, and they increased her morphine dose. I had talked to her each day of those twelve weeks she had previously spent in the hospital and knew how deeply weary she had become from being there. Her words kept echoing in my ears, "I just want to be home," with a longing I could feel like a thud in my chest. The nurses pulled a cot into her room so that John and I could stay with her as we waited, taking turns to close our eyes for a fitful hour at a time. The doctor thought she would pass quickly because of all that her body had been through already.

She held on through Friday night and all day Saturday. When she was still alive on Sunday, we knew it was time to invite her friends to be with her, to let them know what was happening. Twelve of us gathered in that small hospital room, singing songs and sharing stories about my mother. It was a going-away party.

Two hours after everyone left and just John and I were there with her, her blood pressure and heartbeat began to drop, and I knew my mother and I were both at a threshold in our lives. She had clearly been waiting for the party. The slowing beep of the heart monitor sounded in my ears as though it marched her toward death rather than merely recording the journey. I became aware that hope and fear, life and death, and beauty and horror all made a place for themselves in that room among us. And when the beeping became one long sound, I began to wail.

In the days that followed I felt as if I was living in two worlds. One was the world where I pulled myself together and began making all the arrangements needed when someone dies. The other world was the place of deep grief and coming undone.

The night after she died, we went as a family out to dinner to her favorite restaurant. I climbed into the backseat of the car we had rented and found there a small wooden bead in the shape of a butterfly. We had been using the car all week, and this was the first time I had seen this.

As time and my grief continued, more winged creatures kept arriving in the forms of butterflies, birds, and angels.

It seemed as if whenever I didn't think I could go on much further, a feather would cross my path or a bird would soar overhead in such a way that I felt less alone. These moments always lifted me briefly. I felt my mother near, and I felt the presence of something else, a guardian spirit perhaps, whom I could rest into when breathing became hard: an angel of grief who would accompany me through the long days of loss.

GUARDIAN ANGELS

There is a beautiful German movie titled *Wings of Desire* directed by Wim Wenders that was later remade into an American version called *City of Angels*. In one of the scenes, the angels are on a bus with a man traveling who is visibly depressed. One of the angels places a hand on him, infusing him with loving care, and the man's countenance is transformed. He is uplifted.

By the time Jesus arrived into the world, angels had already been an integral part of Jewish belief. Jews believed that every human being had a guardian angel. Most of the psalms were written a thousand years before Jesus was born. Psalm 91:11 says, "For he will command his angels concerning you to guard you in all your ways."

Several of the early church fathers echo this conviction that humans, in all their vulnerability, each have a guardian angel to help support and protect them. Origen, a theologian from the second to third centuries, develops this idea: "All of the faithful in Christ, no matter how small, are helped by an angel,"[1] reflecting this teaching from Jesus's parable of the lost sheep: "Take care that you do not despise one of these little ones; for, I tell you, in heaven their angels continually see the face of my Father in heaven" (Mt 18:10).

Fourth-century theologian and church father St. Basil the Great wrote, "Among the angels, some are set in charge of nations, others are companions of the faithful. . . . It is the teaching of Moses that every believer has an angel to guide him as a teacher and a shepherd."[2] This tradition is echoed in the *Summa Theologica* of St. Thomas Aquinas, where he devotes a lengthy reflection to establishing the existence and function of the guardian angel.[3]

There are many other functions attributed to the angels by these early theologians. They protect the human soul from inner and outer troubles. They help redirect the soul that has gone astray. They support us in our prayer and in connecting to the Divine Presence. The guardian angels were given three titles that correspond to these functions: the angel of peace, Chrysostom; the angel of penitence, Hermas; and the angel of prayer, Tertullian.[4] Angels are a link between heaven and earth.

Writer bell hooks describes angels as bearing witness: "They are the guardian spirits who watch, protect, and guide us throughout our lives. Sometimes they take a human form. At other times they are pure spirit—unseen, unimaginable, just forever present. . . . [They] are able to assist us in our spiritual growth. Unconditional lovers of the human spirit, they were there to help us face reality without fear."[5]

She goes on to write how angels "bring to us the knowledge of how we must journey on the path to love and well-being."[6] Guardian angels are ever-present beings made of spirit who love us unconditionally and help us to walk through life with courage, always toward greater love and wholeness.

You might pause for a moment here and identify somewhere in your life where you feel disturbance to that inner peace. Then identify a place where you feel your heart is out of alignment with the Divine desire for your life. Finally, identify where your prayer has felt dry or connecting to the sacred has felt challenging.

It may be that your response to all three of these is the same core issue in your life. Alternatively, it may be three different things. Or perhaps you are in a fortunate moment of life when things feel steady, aligned, and connected, in which case you might draw upon the memory of these states of being in your past.

The early church theologians would counsel us to call on our guardian angel to help us through these kinds of challenging moments. You could create a simple breath prayer to support you in listening for your angel's wisdom for you. Here is a suggestion for a prayer to say with your breath:

Breathe in: Angel, protect me,
Breathe out: align me, connect me.

Allow some time to let the prayer become woven into your being. Feel these three desires, reach out in your imagination for the sheltering wings of an angel, and draw your arms around yourself to feel this prayer answered. Pope Gregory the Great wrote that angels "refresh us on earth with their ministry and help, because they become fertile in heaven by the dew of contemplation."[8] Feel the sacred dew of refreshment revive your spirit.

Sixth-century Irish monk St. Columba (also known as St. Columcille in Ireland) was the founder of the monastic community at Iona. Peter Stanford writes, "His own authority over his brethren rested on his saintliness, of which one outward sign was said to be his strong relationship with angels. Members of the Iona community would describe seeing Columba standing on a particular grassy knoll on the island talking to strangers."[9] Many of the saints had a special devotion to angels or a moment in their lives when angels visited them. This includes St. Teresa of Avila, who describes her moment of ecstasy with an angel piercing her heart with a blade.[10]

ANGELS AND MUSIC

John Chrysostom, theologian and archbishop of Constantinople (347–407), wrote that the Church's worship is one "that permeates the entire cosmos, in which sun, moon, and all the stars take part. . . . The heaven of angels is . . . the most central, the most spiritual part of the cosmos."[11] He goes on to write that the singing of angels is essential to the Church's praise. In his Rule for monks, St. Benedict describes the Divine Office as an act of singing with the angels. He states the angels needed to be the monks' model not just in worship but also in all of their daily acts and contemplation of the Divine. "We must always be mindful of what the Prophet says: 'Serve God with fear' (Ps 2:11); and again, 'Sing praise wisely' (Ps 46[47]:8); and, 'I will sing praise to You in the sight of the angels' (Ps 137[138]:1). Therefore, let us consider how it becomes us to behave in the sight of God and the angels, and let us stand to sing the psalms in such a way that our minds are in harmony with our voices."[12]

Singing becomes a place to align our bodies and our spirits together through our minds and our voices. The psalmist says they will sing praise to the Divine while in the sight of the angels, which Benedict reiterates as an important principle to remember. Our singing happens within this celestial community.

St. Hildegard of Bingen, a twelfth-century Benedictine abbess and mystic, also saw the presence of angels regularly. She introduced angels into her teaching, especially her first book of visions, *Scivias: Know the Ways of God.*

In one of her visions she saw five "armies" of angels, seeing them in the "secret places in the heights of heaven," and she recognizes them because they "shone with such great brightness." Some of the armies shone so brightly she could not look directly at them. In addition to being radiant with shining light, they were also "singing with marvellous voices all kinds of music about the wonders that God works in blessed souls."[13] She sees them arranged in concentric circles. This vision was later illuminated by her sisters, allowing us to see the array of angels arranged in circles around a blank center, which represents God's mysterious nature. Hildegard suggests that not even the angels can gaze on the Divine face.

Hildegard is known for her compositions of music for the Divine Office, and in her theology, when we sing, we join the choirs of angels who are continually singing in praise of the sacred. In her vision, the angel reminded St. Hildegard that praise was the vocation of all seeking to live a saintly life: "For spirits blessed in the power of God make known in the heavenly places by indescribable sounds their great joy in the works of wonder that God perfects in His saints; by which the latter gloriously magnify God, seeking Him in the depth of sanctity and rejoicing in the joy of salvation."[14]

For Hildegard, it was the Fall in the Garden of Eden that disrupted our original harmony with the Sacred Source of All. It is through singing that we begin to remember this harmony that still exists on a celestial level. Music is the most elevated of all human activities.

Scholar Barbara Newman writes that Hildegard believed "the office of singing pleases God if it is performed with an attentive mind, when in this way we imitate the choirs of angels who are said to sing the Lord's praise without ceasing."[15] The angels call us to remember this original song already flowing through us.

PRACTICE
Cultivating Intuitive Consciousness

Spending time with angels, saints, and ancestors often involves a different kind of communication than our human connections. We can still verbalize our prayers, speak the stories we want to share, and offer up the longings of our hearts, but we don't often hear responses to us in this same way.

To experience communication with the angels and saints surrounding us, we have to cultivate our intuitive ways of knowing. This can include embodied knowing, dreams, synchronicities, paying attention to symbols that repeat, noticing when a song keeps showing up for us, and listening for animal wisdom that often conveys something of the Otherworld to us. This intuitive knowing is often a very foreign way for us to move through the world if we have been trained to prioritize linear thinking, analysis, planning, doing, and efforts to control the direction of our lives. There is certainly a place for this more left-brained, masculine way of being. It helps give shape to the world. But it can become toxic when it is out of balance with the feminine principles of spiral ways of being, honoring cycles and rhythms of creation, yielding, surrendering, feeling deeply, allowing, unfolding, being, and resting into mystery. The feminine honors other ways of knowing, such as the intuitive, symbolic, body, and dream wisdom that comes to us through the natural world, through our radical nighttime surrender, and through moments of reverberation in daily life that manifests in what we call synchronicities.

We can begin to honor the feminine ways of knowing by noticing moments in the day when our bodies offer us wisdom that we can feel. We can start to pay attention to our night dreams, writing them down. We can offer prayers and invite communication from the angels through these modes of the imagination. Then we show up each evening and reflect on the day and pay attention to how what we heard shimmers or whispers of sacred love brushing its wings over us.

MEDITATION
Connecting to a Guardian Angel

Allow some time to breathe deeply and slow down your mind and body. Notice what your body needs for more ease—some shifting or stretching. Then bring your awareness down to your heart center. Enter the sanctuary of the heart where the divine spark of aliveness dwells. Rest here for some time simply being.

Imagine God, the Source of Life, creating a circle of protection around you. Allow a few moments to notice its color. Within this circle you are protected by the Divine Presence in every direction.

Ask the Sacred Source of All to reveal to you your guardian angel. Call on this presence to become visible to you. Open the eyes of your heart.

Try not to force something to happen. Rest in a space of openness, knowing you are being held by the Beloved.

When your guardian angel is revealed, spend some time being in their company. Notice their color, energy, and quality of presence. Ask them for their name. Rest together for a while. See how your body responds.

If nothing seems to come, continue to rest in the arms of the Beloved. If there is no visual sense of presence, notice if perhaps there is a felt sense in your body.

Once you feel connected in this sanctuary space, you might ask your guardian angel a question or share something on your heart. Then listen for any wisdom offered.

Ask your guardian angel if there is a particular sign in your daily life you can pay attention to, to be assured of their presence with you. See what the response is. It might be through a sound, a symbol, or through a felt sense in your body.

Make a commitment to tend more diligently to their presence in your daily life.

Give thanks for this time together. Allow several deep breaths and then slowly transition back to the room you are in.

CREATIVE EXPLORATION
Poem Writing

Read the poem below by Luci Shaw twice slowly. Notice which lines shimmer for you as you read.

> Some days I notice angels everywhere—
> light glancing through windows, flying
> through stained glass as if through air.
> A human ear shaped like a wing,
> curiously curving to admit a flare
> of sound, tells me of angels listening
> to my listening, even as I sing.
> What is that vagrant cloud, that glistening?
> Often in the blue of heaven a trail
> of light from a plane to me appears
> as a heavenly body playing there
> beyond my grasping. Or, at night, the tail-
> light of a truck sends a red spark
> like some twinkly being in the dark
> trailing her glory robe in sight
> of stationary sightseers. Yesterday, morning light
> and over the marsh a winged flight,
> another view—Gabriel, or a Great Blue?
> But often, nightly, through the skylight
> stars multiply like silver sand. And near to far
> I link myself again with, Oh—there!
> One bright, angelic, particular star.[16]

Write your own poem inspired by Shaw's words. You might begin with her first line, "Some days I notice angels everywhere," and then see where your imagination takes you. Create a list of all the places where you have had angelic encounters, from the most mundane to the most spectacular.

Rather than beginning with Shaw's first line, you can instead begin with one of the lines that shimmered for you. Write a poem in honor of all the ways the angels are present to you just beyond your awareness.

Blessing of Your Guardian Angel

This blessing comes as a love note
being scrawled across the bright sky
with ink of feathers gliding,
a gentle whisper when you feel stretched thin,
when loneliness swallows you,
when your heart is unsettled,
or you feel utterly and completely lost.
Breathe once slowly, then again,
and with a third deep breath, close your eyes
and attune to the warmth of sheltering wings.
Feel your body yield into this loving presence.
When prayer feels impossible,
may your guardian angel
sing the sweetest sounds,
kindling a new song in your own heart.
Feel your spirit lifted, courage wrapping
itself around you, your inner compass
guiding you to where you most need to be.
Feel your soul infused with the grace of peace.
See the span of the angel's wings
weaving together heaven and earth,
on a loom of Love,
lifting your voice in song
to join with the celestial harmony.

May you pay attention
to shimmering moments
and know your guardian angel
has beckoned you to pause,
to know this as gift.
May they bring you back
into alignment with the Holy desire for your life
and refresh you on the meadow of your days,
bless you with sacred dew.

3

WRESTLING WITH ANGELS

The same night he got up and took his two wives, his two maids, and his eleven children, and crossed the ford of the Jabbok. He took them and sent them across the stream, and likewise everything that he had. Jacob was left alone; and a man wrestled with him until daybreak. When the man saw that he did not prevail against Jacob, he struck him on the hip socket; and Jacob's hip was put out of joint as he wrestled with him. Then he said, "Let me go, for the day is breaking." But Jacob said, "I will not let you go, unless you bless me." So he said to him, "What is your name?" And he said, "Jacob." Then the man said, "You shall no longer be called Jacob, but Israel, for you have striven with God and with humans, and have prevailed."

—Genesis 32:22–28

Several months after my mother died, I heard the story of Jacob wrestling with the angel in church one Sunday. I had heard this story proclaimed many times before, but this time was different. The story became personal to me in a way it had never been before. There are many layers to this powerful narrative, and scholars debate whether Jacob was wrestling with an angel or perhaps even God's very self. Regardless of who Jacob wrestled with, at that moment the story spoke directly to my grief.

During my time of intense loss I began to question everything I thought I knew about who God was and what faith was. I didn't realize at the time I was in a dark night of the soul; I only saw it in retrospect. In the dark night experience, everything that felt secure and comforting and certain is suddenly stripped away. For a long season I was in a wrestling match with God and the angels. I wanted so desperately to know why death is woven into the fabric of this world and why we have to lose those we love. I wanted to know why we have to endure so much sorrow and suffering again and again. The wrestling can feel like a long, dark night when the sun may never rise again.

Perhaps what made this story land in a new way for me was that, at the time, I was dealing with hip pain of unknown causes. The story suddenly illuminated the reason, at least on one level of understanding: I had been wrestling so long and so hard that my hip socket had been dislocated. My sense of being "out of joint" was deeply embodied for me in my hip pain. At the same time, though, I was beginning to see the faint glimmer of the sun's rising in the east finally. Anyone who has gone through their own journey of deep and conscious grief knows the way it carves out a deep well of compassion in you for others. When you know the sorrows of your life so profoundly, that knowledge can't help but connect you to others in a kinship of mourning.

I was still angry with God or life or the world, whatever had woven death, and therefore grief, into the way things were. And so, I said if things had to be that way, then I demanded a blessing. I demanded that there be some gift from it all—not in a way that would deny the pain or cancel it out, but something that would help make it somewhat easier to carry.

In the poem "Wrestling Jacob," the eighteenth-century Methodist minister Charles Wesley writes, "Speak to my heart, in blessings speak; Be conquered by my instant prayer; / Speak, or thou never hence shalt move / And tell me if thy name be Love." Later in the poem he writes in the affirmative: "Thy nature and thy name is Love."[1] It demands a great deal of imagination and openheartedness to see the love at the heart of the wrestling, to trust that amid the struggles, life still pulses with compassion and lavish care for our well-being.

Mary Oliver has a poem titled "Angels" in which she writes that angels can be visible at any moment if you can open your eyes in a different way to see them. She describes this as a form of "second level" vision.[2] Perhaps ironically, it is spending time in the darkness, in the landscape of unknowing, and not grasping for certainty but letting ourselves be undone by the mystery of it all, that we learn to see in a different way. It is in the long wrestling match that we learn that our encounters with angels are not always about sweetness and light. Sometimes they demand something bigger from us, a way of seeing God beyond all the confines we have created.

The blessings that came from that season of life have been many. Not only has it widened my capacity for compassion for others and my ability to sit with them in their own anguish without flinching, but it also initiated me into a deeper journey of the soul. "Jacob's struggle with the angel provides the ultimate transformation. It is one of the richest metaphors of the Bible. It entails numerous levels of meanings, all echoing transformation."[3] The dark night moves us toward a different relationship with the Divine, one where we let go of our own limited understanding of God and all that we think we know, all the boxes we try to cram God into, and rest into the wider mystery of things. The Divine Presence becomes one that grieves with us, laments over our losses, holds us, and slowly guides us to new ways to become gifts to the community. Our agony is transmuted into medicine for others.

This is a blessing we claim for ourselves. We demand it because we know we need it to carry on in ways that bring solace to a world in pain. In the process of receiving our blessing, like Jacob, we also receive a new name. Jacob's name was given to him, and it heralded his future as the father of a community of people. Our name might be hidden in the secret recesses of our hearts, or it might come through the recognition of someone in our lives of the gifts we now carry. Wise one, companion, guide, seer, and wounded healer might be some of the ways we begin to see ourselves and how others see us. We stop looking to explain things. Instead, we learn to trust our growing sense of the sacred presence and how it is the ground of everything. This Source of Love leads us to love and more love.

Jacob's Ladder

Before he wrestles with an angel, Jacob has a dream one night, his head resting on a stone: "And he dreamed that there was a ladder set up on the earth, the top of it reaching to heaven; and the angels of God were ascending and descending on it" (Gn 28:12). Following this image of the ascent and descent of angels, he is promised by God the land that he is resting on, as well as the abundance of his lineage. When Jacob wakes, he is in a state of awe and wonder and declares the place as "the gate of heaven" (v. 17).

Jacob has been granted a vision of the possibilities that lie before him and an invitation to consider his own spiritual growth as a movement up the ladder or stairway. God has planted the seeds, but Jacob must do the work of transformation. He can choose to practice the way of life, or he can continue to choose the way of death. He is crossing a threshold into a new relationship to God and to his own unfolding path in life.

How often do we have an experience of illumination in our lives, a moment of clarity about who we are and how we should move forward, only to then find ourselves again in a wrestling match with the Divine? This was the case for Jacob. The night Jacob wrestles with the angel is the night he was heading to meet his brother, Esau, who sought revenge for Jacob's betrayals. In meeting with Esau, Jacob had a chance to put his moment of transformation into practice, choosing the path of either life or death.

Enlarged by Defeat

In his poem "The Man Watching," the German-language poet Rainer Maria Rilke writes about the angels of the Hebrew stories and how we are called to allow ourselves to embrace our vulnerability and the possibility of defeat. He writes how what we choose to fight with is small but what interrupts our lives to fight us is always great. These are the last two stanzas:

> What we defeat are small things,
> and this success makes us small.
> The eternal and immense
> does not want to be bent by us.
> This is the Angel who appeared
> to the wrestlers of the Hebrew Scriptures:
> when his adversaries' sinews
> stretched long like steel in battle,
> he felt them beneath his fingers
> like the strings of low melodies.
> Whoever was overcome by this Angel,
> who so often refrains from fighting,
> they walk away upright and lifted
> made great by that hard hand,
> nestling and shaping them.
> Victories do not tempt them.
> Their way to grow: being utterly defeated
> by the eternally greater being.[4]

Rilke is speaking here to the reality that our defeats in life, our willingness to wrestle with the big questions and admit our sometimes helplessness, also bring growth. They paradoxically help to expand our being.

Amma Theodora, one of the Desert Mothers, offers us this story: "Let us strive to enter by the narrow gate. Just as the trees, if they have not stood before the winter's storms cannot bear fruit, so it is with us; this present age is a storm and it is only through many trials and temptations that we can obtain an inheritance in the kingdom of heaven."[5]

Several years ago in Arizona, a biodome was constructed to reproduce Earth's ecosystems and study them. They discovered, however, that as the trees grew, they were spindly and weak; eventually, they toppled over. The cause was the lack of wind within the dome. Because there was no wind inside for the trees to fight against as they grew, they did not develop the sturdiness needed to grow fully. Their roots never needed to reach deep into the soil to become firmly planted.

Amma Theodora offers us the same wisdom from her experience in the desert. The trees must stand before winter's storms to be able to bear fruit. So must we wrestle with the angels of our lives to grow in endurance and also bring forth the gifts that were planted within us. There is no easy pathway through life. Those who deny the need to wrestle with our experiences of uncertainty and unfairness often develop a fundamentalist approach to life, which falsely offers easy answers and a sense of control. One of the many gifts of wrestling with the angels is moving more deeply into our capacity to hold paradox, to embrace mystery, to endure the times of waiting and vigil that can be so challenging, and to honor the suffering of ourselves and others.

PRACTICE
Patient Endurance

There is a Greek word, *hupomone*, which essentially means patient enduring, steadfastness, and perseverance, to stay with whatever is happening, to sit there and simply stay put. This was a core practice of the Desert Mothers and Fathers who stayed in their monastic "cells"—which might have been a cave or other dwelling—but was also a metaphor for staying with their own experience. This means not running away not only physically but also emotionally. We are always running away from ourselves, our impulses, our sorrows, and our compulsions in a variety of ways through our desire for distraction and relief. Abba Moses taught, "Go sit in your cell, and your cell will teach you everything."[6]

Hupomone is similar to the central Benedictine concept of stability. On one level it calls monks to a lifetime commitment within a particular community: "From this day [of his monastic vows] he is no longer free to leave the monastery, nor to shake from his neck the yoke of the rule which, in the course of so prolonged a period of reflection, he was free to either reject or accept" (*The Rule of St. Benedict*, 58.15). St. Benedict required his monks to commit to a monastery for their whole lives so they would be encouraged not to run away when things got challenging.

On another level, the call is to not run away from conflict or difficulty during our lives. Stability and steadfastness demand that we stay with difficult experiences and remain present to the discomfort they create in us. Though, as other desert sayings invite us to consider, staying in one place for our lives does not guarantee that we will also be committed to an internal staying with our experience. Within the cell we will encounter boredom and loneliness. Our thoughts will begin to distract us and take us away from our experience.

Amma Syncletica, another of the Desert Mothers, warns other monks to not go running from place to place when things grow difficult where you are: "If you find yourself in a monastery do not go to another place, for that will harm you a great deal. Just as the bird who abandons the eggs she was sitting on prevents them from hatching, so the monk or the nun grows cold and their faith dies when they go from one place to another."[7]

The eggs require the bird to stay there and keep them warm, rather than flying away in search of new experiences or vistas. Our restlessness is the cause of so much internal fleeing. When we grow uncomfortable with what we are experiencing, we think stuffing it down or moving on will mean we don't have to deal with it. Stability and patience call us to stay *with* our experience, to be fully present to whatever is happening within us. Moving about from place to place can be a form of distraction as we place our energies outside of us. If the cell represents the place where we encounter God, patience speaks to the time within which our encounter will happen. God's time is different than ours, and the work of the cell is slow. Angels are present with us to help us endure.

We move about in our minds as well; even when the body is still, we let our minds carry us far back into the past or into the future. My own inclination is to live in the future, to always be planning ahead. My organized self loves calendars and to-do lists. While these are important aspects of my work, they can also become a way of avoiding my own experience in the current moment. I find myself sometimes so focused on checking things off my list or figuring things out that I abandon myself in this moment by not staying present.

Our breath can be a tremendous ally in the practice of patience and perseverance. It can help us to withstand emotional pain and distress, and it can bring us present to this moment when we want to flee into future dreaming to avoid what is happening right now.

MEDITATION
Remembering

This meditation is inspired by St. Ignatius of Loyola's Examen. Spend time in preparation for this meditation by looking through old photographs if possible, but consciously revisiting experiences in your memory works as well. Then find a quiet space, slow down your breathing, and drop inward into your imagination. Reflect back on your life, and imagine that you are walking through each decade as if on a physical pilgrimage. Honor the journeys you have made. Pay attention to those moments of grace and ease when you felt a profound sense of consolation and love in your life. Let each God-kissed moment rise up, and spend time savoring it and offering a prayer of gratitude for it.

Then shift your awareness and walk through your memories again. This time pay attention to those moments of challenge and discomfort, perhaps even desolation. Let each moment rise up, and honor its role as part of your life story. See if there is anyone you would like to forgive for this experience, including yourself. Ask for God's companionship in this journey of tenderness and remembering.

To complete the experience, bring your awareness back to the present moment and notice what you have discovered about yourself by remembering these times of both grace and challenge. Take some time to name the gifts of this pilgrimage of memory.

Memory can be a powerful source for our prayer and contemplation. To "re-member" means to make whole again. When we forget parts of our own story, we cut off parts of our life from the wholeness of who we are. Integration happens when we begin to gather all the exiled parts of ourselves, all those memories that were too embarrassing, too painful, or too humbling to examine at the time.

Begin by deepening your breath and bringing yourself fully present to the moment. Draw your awareness down to your heart center and feel your feet on the floor. Imagine you are connected to the earth beneath your feet and feel the support of the ground and the chair you are sitting on.

Spend some quiet time in reflection on the moments of your life that have been a struggle, where you felt as if you were wrestling with greater forces than you. Let each experience arise and allow some space to enter into the experience again from a different place in your life. Consider the questions it raised for you about God and the nature of life, suffering, and death.

Notice whether this life experience has a feeling of completion, meaning that you allowed time and space for it to affect you and then for you to integrate what happened. If you find that you didn't, make a commitment to remember it now and in the coming days, bring a heart of compassion to yourself.

After you have spent some time embodying these moments again, consider the ways some of these experiences might have strengthened your capacity for presence or compassion to others. What were the blessings of this time, if any? If you are not able to identify or remember a blessing, demand that the angel give you a blessing now and listen for a response.

Sometimes we wrestle and are left defeated. Not all losses bear fruit or bring blessing. Honor those experiences that still feel like deep grief without consolation. Make space for these dark night times that do not have any sense of resolution. Resist the urge to make meaning that has not yet unfolded.

Spend some time with a journal to record your experiences. Make note of the memories you want to return to and continue to work with.

CREATIVE EXPLORATION
Midrash with Jacob and the Angel

Midrash is an ancient practice of the Jewish tradition. Rabbis wrote Midrash to help explain problems they encountered in the biblical texts such as inconsistencies or missing voices. These stories form an important part of the Jewish sacred literature.

In Judaism, scripture is sometimes described as black fire on white fire. Black fire is the words on the page. Midrash illuminates the white fire, the spaces between the words that are written. Through Midrash we explore the gaps in the story, the missing voices, the silences, and the wondering that is sparked.

St. Ignatius of Loyola, a Spanish mystic and founder of the Jesuit order of priests, offered a way of praying the scriptures through the imagination that has much kinship to Midrash. In what is often referred to as Ignatian prayer of the imagination, we are invited into the cracks and spaces of the story to see what is revealed to us.

Ignatius believed that our imagination, senses, and feelings were holy vessels and portals into understanding the sacred. He invites us to read a text prayerfully, and then to imagine stepping into the story ourselves, seeing, hearing, tasting, smelling, and feeling what it is like to be in the scene. He suggests we have conversations with the characters to see what they might say to us in what is known as a *colloquy*. This prayer is about entering ourselves within the story, both body and soul, and seeing what we encounter. These words of the sacred texts are meant to be alive, and because they are archetypal, they can speak to human experience across time.

Both of these practices, Midrash and Ignatian prayer, embrace the profound significance biblical stories can have for us personally when we allow ourselves to not just read at a distance but to also enter into them with all of our senses attuned. Rather than just sitting back and hearing them read to us from a lectern at church, we are called to dive into the story fully and see what we discover. There is an acknowledgment of the truth that can arise in our imaginative engagement with sacred texts.

Read the scripture story of Jacob wrestling all night with the angel that opens this chapter again. Read the text through slowly. Imagine that you are experiencing the story right now; it is not some distant mythical account but a story meant to become alive for you. Allow a few moments of silent pause and then begin to notice where your attention and curiosity are drawn.

Let yourself enter the scene with all of your senses engaged. What do you see, taste, smell, hear, and feel? Allow some time for these to each reveal themselves.

You might have a conversation with the angel or with Jacob or with an animal you imagine was a witness to this event. You might imagine how each character was feeling: What was their desire or longing? Put them in dialogue with one another. Notice your own questions arising and pose them. What wisdom do they have to offer to you?

Feel free to write in prose or poetry form. However the words emerge is perfect.

A Blessing for Wrestling with Angels

You have known
the long nights of wrestling
with mysterious beings,
your breath hard and fast,
your heart pounding
like furious wings.
The dark seems to stretch forever,
and you wonder how long
you will be in the grip
of this powerful stranger,
how long you will have to hold on.
Then slowly the black pool above you
gives way to violet, fuchsia, tangerine,
and you feel your hip wounded,

throbbing, pulsing with pain,
know you will be limping
for many years to come,
but before letting go
you make your demand:
Bless me, your voice thunders,
and the being erupts into golden light,
so glad that you had finally asked.
A new name sings out through the ether
like the most exquisite melody,
a chant for the new season ahead,
a name which reminds you of the long night
and how you would not relent,
how courage and hope and stubbornness
carried you through.
May you find endurance
when you are lost and disoriented,
may your wounds be reminders
of your willingness to struggle,
may you demand a blessing
as light begins its breaking,
and may your new name
call forth the gifts already inside you,
an offering of love to others
still wrestling in the dark.

Part Two

SAINTS

4

WE ARE ALL CALLED TO BE SAINTS AND MYSTICS

The Christian of the future will be a mystic, or [s]he will not exist at all.

—Karl Rahner, *Theological Investigations*

At the heart of mysticism—no matter which tradition we are speaking of—is a profound sense of God's intimate and transforming presence in our lives, which always expands our capacity for love. I am often asked how a person knows whether they have had a genuine encounter with God, and my response is that if the experience leads to greater love for other, for self, or for God, then we can know that we have met the Holy One in some way. We experience these moments of connection through our own practice and through opening our hearts to listen. But equally as important is through divine grace, which always extends out toward us, always seeking to be in communion with us. Sometimes mystical connection is not what we are seeking, but it is visited upon us regardless.

41

Fourth-century Orthodox mystic Gregory of Nyssa talked about *epektasis*, which is a Greek word meaning "stretching forth always," based on Philippians 3:13, where Paul talks about always stretching forward toward God. It refers to the continual yearning, which is never satisfied in this life. We all have this core desire to reach toward God, but we often mistake it for something else and try to fill it with things like drinking, shopping, drug use, or any other addictive behavior.

While some have sudden moments of grace or epiphanies into the divine nature and call, like St. Paul at Damascus, those tend to be the exception in the mystical life. Mystics commit themselves to extensive practice in prayer and meditation, spiritual reading, and meeting with a mentor or soul friend in an ongoing way. As theologian Bernard McGinn says, "Mysticism is a process. It requires preparation. It also involves a moment of some kind of direct consciousness of God. And then it involves the effects of all the elements of the process on that person's life. It's meant to be transformative—to make people different, both in themselves and in how they relate to other people. I prefer the word 'consciousness' to 'experience' because consciousness involves thinking and loving and decision-making, as well as experience and feeling."[1]

The paradox of the mystical experience is that it requires preparation and the discipline of showing up for an encounter with the Divine, but ultimately, the experience is grace and freely given. We do not earn it or work hard enough to achieve it. We open our hearts to it, and grace explodes. It transforms our hearts by expanding our capacity for love.

Way of Knowing and Unknowing

Mysticism involves both the cataphatic way of knowing and the apophatic way of unknowing. Through the cataphatic we come to know God through images, art, music, nature, and relationships—all the physical expressions of the Divine incarnate. Everything we know through the senses of taste, smell, touch, hearing, and sight can lead us to a vision of the sacred pulsing in all of creation.

But equally so we come to know God through the apophatic, through darkness, mystery, silence, and unknowing—acknowledging that God's mystery is always vaster than what we can imagine. Any name points to the divine nature, but it also constrains God by placing the sacred in a box. If that name becomes the whole of our understanding of God, we greatly limit our vision. We always have to hold this tension between our knowing and our unknowing.

McGinn describes a third principle, which he calls "hyperphatic": "God is beyond both affirmation and negation, insofar as we know these, because we do so from a limited, finite perspective. So according to Pseudo-Dionysius and many other mystics, you eventually reach the level of what I call the hyperphatic: God is beyond both affirmation and negation in a realm that we really cannot talk about. We talk around it, and silence is where we finally wind up, in adoring silence of the mystery."[2]

Ultimately the mystic is one who can hold the paradox of the divine nature—who can celebrate the sacred presence in hummingbirds and rivers, in dog whiskers and in granite, but also knows that God is all of these things and beyond them. Until we can come to that third way, we will be living out of a false dualism of all or nothing.

It is this ability to hold paradox that allows the mystic to be present to the terrible suffering in the world while also seeing God's shimmering presence everywhere. This ability to bring the profundity of love into a broken world is the hallmark of a mystic who is living into their sainthood.

Becoming a Saint

The specifically Christian concept of the Communion of Saints is linked with Paul's teaching that in Christ Christians form a single body (see Romans 12:4–13 and 1 Corinthians 12:12–27). He refers to a group of those who are especially virtuous and serve God with great devotion. During the early years of Christianity, when martyrdom was common, those who refused to denounce their faith became saints. But once this period ended, the name "saint" became linked to specific people who had died, who during their lifetimes lived in a particularly intimate way with God, serving the community out of that love.

Only those who died became saints. Those who lived exemplary lives of virtue were assumed to transition in death to the heavenly realm. However, because they had walked among the living, in human bodies, with human struggles, they offered a more tangible connection to the sacred for many than angels did. The stories of their lives, filled with temptation, suffering, doubt, and ultimately a deep and abiding faith and intimacy with the Divine, meant that they could become role models for how to navigate this earthly world. While for some, the virtue of the saints may seem unreachable, their humanity offered a balance to this reality. Being a saint also meant being a part of this wider communion that stretches across both earth and heaven.

It was only in 1234 that the Roman Church took control of the process of becoming a saint and created a formal, bureaucratic process that persists to current times. Prior to that it was a much more spontaneous and localized process to confer sainthood.

In the second millennium, the veneration of the saints became more central to the daily life of the Church. Shrines appeared across Europe housing relics and attracting pilgrims. Devotions and processions took place on feast days, and miraculous cures were ascribed to the saints. Choosing a saint at Confirmation provided people with a guide in life.

We Are All Called to Be Saints

So far what I have written about saints is drawing on the Catholic Church's definition of what an official saint is. Prior to the Church creating a rigid and defined canonization process, there was a wider honoring of who could be considered a saint. Ireland is called the "Land of Saints and Scholars" because, in that early medieval period before the Roman Church took hold, the localized practice was to call anyone a saint who had lived a holy life. It was a more organic process that rose out of the experience of a specific community's relationship with a person. This understanding of what it means to live in a holy way came from the place and the people the holy person touched, rather than being imposed by a religious hierarchy. In contrast, becoming a saint now is a long and expensive process, which must have the power and resources of a religious order to carry it forward.

St. Paul writes that we are all "called to be holy" (1 Cor 1:2). We all know people in our lives who live from a stance of love, kindness, generosity, patience, and abiding presence to the sacred and all the ways it is made manifest in our world. These are the everyday saints we honor. They may be our neighbors, our coworkers, our aunts, or our brothers, but their lives witness to another way of being in the world. They may have passed on or may still be walking this earth. So when I write about honoring saints in this book, I refer to the acknowledged saints, such as Francis, Hildegard, Benedict, Augustine, and Teresa. But I also want to encourage a wider vision and consider those in our lives who have shown us what it means to love generously in a world that is often hard to love. These may also be people we have not met, but they inspire us through their poetry or music, through their commitment to social justice and the poor, or through other pathways.

Essentially, saints embody certain qualities, the first of which is love and the second is humility. Saints are able to set aside their own plans and what they think is the best path forward and have a practice of listening for holy direction. They take risks and follow the Divine's lead into new ways of serving others. They are also fully human and struggle with all the things that humans do, all the limitations we encounter through body and spirit.

Cultivating mystical presence in the world requires periods of retreat and time spent in silence and solitude as the early desert monks and Jesus practiced, who often disappeared for a while to restore. But ultimately, this solitary replenishment is in service of the wider community. Indeed, there are some who live cloistered lives as hermits or anchorites, but even in these cases they are praying for the world, and often people come to seek them out for spiritual guidance and wisdom.

Mysticism is a consciousness affecting every level of our being. It is not simply an experience or feeling. Through these encounters, our ways of being in the world are slowly transformed. It becomes how we see everything around us.

In the quote that opens this chapter, theologian Karl Rahner noted that Christians in the future will either be mystics or cease to be anything at all. Without this lived experience of the Divine and without this cultivation of love, religion becomes dry and empty, lived purely for the institution rather than inner transformation. It loses its vitality. St. Benedict described conversion as a practice of lifelong transformation. We are never done falling more in love with God, with the world, and with one another. As long as we are alive, there is always more love to pour out. In the process, we may inspire others to deepen into that place of love and generosity as well.

PRACTICE
Called to Be Holy

How do we embody and live out St. Paul's call to be holy? How do we embody the witness of the saints, which is to live into their full holiness? Thomas Merton wrote, "For me to be a saint means to be myself."[3] While this sounds so simple on the surface, we know how challenging it is, how many obstacles we set before ourselves, how many layers of fear and resistance have built up over the years, how much our egos are attached to being viewed in a certain way, and what images and identities we are grasping to hold on to.

As you sit with these words from Merton, I invite you to listen for this call to be fully yourself and how best to get out of your own way. What are the masks you wear? The ways you pretend around others to be something you are not? What is your heart's deep desire? What would you be doing if you weren't afraid of the judgment of others? Let your heart soften into suppleness, readying yourself to receive a new insight, a new vision. Listen for the wisdom that arises in the stillness.

This feels so challenging and is such a lifelong journey. We can only practice our holiness and never perfect it, meaning we will stumble along the way because we are human. We can only ask each day, What is one thing I can do to live more deeply in alignment with my deeper, truer self? Practicing holiness means recognizing that holiness is not a destination at which we arrive once and for all.

MEDITATION
Communion of Saints

Begin by slowing down your breath. Breathing slowly and deeply, let your breath carry your awareness from your mind, the place where your thoughts clamor for attention, to the heart, the place where you are open to resting in mystery. Experience the shift from needing to figure things out to dropping into a place where there is nothing that needs doing; you can simply be.

Open yourself to the presence of the Divine here in the sanctuary of the heart. Allow a few moments to be held in that embrace, breathing together.

Imagine there is a beautiful fire burning within you, a fire that represents all the love and passion you feel for the world and the world feels for you and your gifts. You are sitting by it under the night sky with a million stars glittering and a sliver of a moon.

Slowly emerging in the distance, out of the darkness of night, you see dozens of people coming. They are all dressed differently from various time periods and places, but what they all have in common is a radiant glow about them, the kind of glow that comes from a sense of intimate connection to the Holy One, and an ongoing sense of peace and joyfulness amid all of life's struggles.

You realize this is the Communion of Saints coming to gather here with you around the fire. You recognize some as saints you know and are familiar with, and others are friends you have yet to meet. Some come forward and embrace you, saying how much they have been looking forward to this time together.

They sit in concentric circles that spiral out from the fire at the center, and there is the most beautiful singing that emerges while others join in. You somehow know the song that is being sung, and you find your voice merged with this incredible chorus.

One of the saints you recognize stands up, turns toward you, and asks, What are the prayers on your heart right now for the world and your community? You pause to listen to your heart's longings and begin to name the issues causing great suffering in the world that are breaking your heart.

As you speak your prayers aloud, you hear a murmur of prayers arising from this gathering, and you can feel the love growing and being sent out to various corners of the world. With every place and situation you name, you can see the love of thousands being amplified and magnified, showering down into every corner of violence or hunger or need.

When you have finished naming the prayers you are holding, another song starts to be sung, and you find yourself weeping at its beauty and power. You rest there a while, being held in this great communion of loving souls.

After resting in this communion, you realize it is time to head back, and you offer a deep bow of gratitude in all directions toward this gathering. They raise their hands in blessing over you and remind you they are there waiting for you to call them toward you whenever you need the support.

You receive this gift of love and blessing and breathe it all in deeply. Continue breathing slowly and deeply, and very gently bring yourself back to the room you are in. Allow some time to journal anything you want to remember.

CREATIVE EXPLORATION
Creating an Altar for the Saints and a Calendar of Feast Days

This creative exploration is similar to the one suggested in Chapter 1, where you were invited to create an angel altar and calendar of feast days.

You might decide to create a second altar to honor the saints, or you might decide to expand your angel altar to include the saints there as well.

Decide first if you would like to have your altar honor one particular saint or the Communion of Saints in general. Spend some time with this question, and ask the Spirit for guidance. Which would feel more helpful and supportive in this season of your life? Do you have someone in mind, whether a canonized saint or an unofficial one who has affected you by how they lived their life?

If it is one of the saints from the Catholic, Orthodox, or Celtic churches, you can search online to find images of them. Let this be a prayerful experience of gathering images into a folder on your computer. Icons have always been revered as windows into the Divine Presence. Icons of saints help us to connect to them as human beings who walked this earth. Sometimes you can order saint cards or small plaques, and you might want to consider doing so for your altar. You could also just print an image or two on a color printer at home or have the images printed at a local print shop, being mindful of copyright.

You might select a certain saint to be the patron saint of the work you do, one who can hold you in prayer and care as you labor. Another saint might be chosen as the patron of family life if you are a caregiver to children or elders. Perhaps another might be the patron saint of a creative pursuit you have, such as writing or painting.

If you want to honor an unofficial saint, gather some photos of them in a similarly prayerful way and print the ones that shimmer for you the most, meaning the images that reveal some dimension of the person you want to especially remember or honor. If you don't have photos available, then consider creating your own sacred drawing or find symbols for them.

I also like to include the canine companions I have loved dearly in the Communion of Saints. Thomas Merton wrote that the "pale flowers of the dogwood outside this window are saints . . . the bass and trout hiding in the deep pools of the river are canonized by their beauty and their strength. The lakes hidden among the hills are saints, and the sea too is a saint who praises God without interruption in her majestic dance."[4] I had an artist friend create a beautiful triptych for me, which honors Duke and Tune, two of our beloved furry four-legged saints who taught me much about devotion and presence to the moment.

Ask the saint to be with you as you continue to build your altar. Gather symbols that evoke a sense of the saint's qualities. A stone could represent strength and solidity of foundation. A feather could represent lightness, and as St. Hildegard says, being "a feather on the breath of God." If your saint has a particular object or creature connected to them, see if you can find a way to symbolize this. Include a candle and perhaps some incense to light. Incense can be a powerful way to feel connected between the worlds.

On your calendar add in the feast days of the saints you have chosen to guide you. Our community, Abbey of the Arts, has a whole series of dancing monks and mystics whom we consider to be the patron saints of our community. These patrons range from the Desert Mothers and Fathers to the Celtic saints, to St. Benedict and St. Hildegard, and to more modern figures such as the poet Rainer Maria Rilke and activist Howard Thurman. You can search to see whether the saints you have chosen have an official feast day. If not, then you could include their birth dates or death dates in your calendar. I use a digital calendar, which allows me to have these feast days set to reappear every year. On those days, spend some extra time in prayer with their spirits. Imagine yourself journeying together and the wisdom they want to share with you.

A Blessing to Become Yourself

This blessing sits in the quiet moments with you
and blesses the longings you feel,
stretching forth toward a vast presence,
a desire to know yourself as holy.
It whispers Merton's reminder:
to be a saint is to be yourself,
and each day you try to release
all that is false and untrue.
Some days you know what it is
to see love everywhere,
to be astounded by the way light shifts,
to feel your heart lifted with a flock of swans,

to rest in the smile of a loved one,
to know aliveness in the pulsing of blood
or in spring's explosion of color.
Some days it is the silence of the heart
and the fertile darkness which kindle love.
These memories become manna,
the sustenance that carries you forward
when life aches, when everything is raw,
or when you've lost feeling altogether.
They are like a muscle strengthened,
so when you find a mountain ahead,
you know you will climb slowly, step by step.
This blessing comes like a summons,
so that when you encounter cruelty,
you shower kindness,
when you are met with greed,
you shower generosity and service,
and when the world feels filled with hatefulness,
Love arises from every aspect of who you are.
You walk through this life with open hands,
your doubts, hopes, despair, grief, anger,
joy, the not knowing all welcome,
but you let Love be your compass,
let it guide you toward a more beautiful world
which you build with kindred spirits,
moment by moment, always unfolding,
both incomplete and fully here all at once.

5

EMBODIED LOVE

And I saw the seven angels who stand before God, and
seven trumpets were given to them.
Another angel with a golden censer came and stood
at the altar; he was given a great quantity of incense
to offer with the prayers of all the saints on the golden
altar that is before the throne. And the smoke of the
incense, with the prayers of the saints, rose before God
from the hand of the angel.

—Revelation 8:2–4

Several years ago when I lived in Seattle, I worked for the Ignatian
Spirituality Center. One of my responsibilities was coordinating the
annual Lenten Novena of Grace, a nine-day preached retreat. To be
honest, when I started the position, the idea of a novena felt quite
foreign to me, perhaps a bit old-fashioned. But this is where I fell in
love with experiencing a novena in community. Through nine days of
intentional prayer together, I saw how it could transform people and me.

There were two services daily—midday and evening—so people
could choose which fit best into their daily rhythm of life. As a part of
the service, we offered prayers at the end with relics, which are tiny
fragments of the remains of saints, in this case Ignatian ones such as

St. Francis Xavier and St. Ignatius of Loyola. The Catholic tradition is nothing if not incarnational, in touch with the embodiment of human life. I find something so beautiful about this honoring of the physical, tangible connection to the Communion of Saints.

It was my responsibility to walk over to Seattle University where the relics were kept to pick them up. They are housed in small glass and metal cases with the name of the saint on them and with the relic itself contained within, no larger than the head of a pin. I was responsible each year for those nine days for those irreplaceable objects. I remember my first year going to get them; I was handed a small box that held them snugly inside, and I placed it gently into my backpack and headed to work. As I walked, I was aware of the unusual circumstances of my situation, wandering the streets of Seattle with the remains of the saints jostling in my backpack.

On my way to work, I stopped at Walgreens to pick up some pain reliever for a headache that had been building all morning. I walked through the aisles between mascara and foundation, toothpaste and deodorant, with the relics at my side. I headed to the pain relief section and stood in front of the massive array of choices to soothe the aches of human living. I wanted to make my selection quickly to get the relics to their destination. Then I realized in a moment of grace and clarity, What better place for the saints to be than there in Walgreens? These holy persons who walked the earth and had their own transformations also had their own physical aches and pains. Ignatius of Loyola knew intimately the profound physical pain of injury and also the doorway it can sometimes offer into something deeper.

Suddenly they were standing there with me, Francis and Ignatius. They were blessing me with my headache and backpack as I stood there, holding my cell phone, wallet, keys, and the sacred bone fragments. They were blessing each bottle of pills, praying that those who purchased them would find relief in both body and spirit. They were blessing the other people who gathered for a brief few moments in that space with me—the elderly man shuffling along slowly looking for a card to express some heartfelt wish to a loved one, the young girl who was skipping through the aisles asking her tired mother for candy, and the tired mother who was just laid off from her part-time work that was keeping ends together and now looking at lipstick colors to grasp at some sense of her own beauty for a moment. I joined them in their blessings, singing them in my heart, showering them on everyone I saw.

I brought my bottle up to the counter. The woman checking out my purchase was cheerful, asking if I had seen their special on eye cream. I wanted to ask her if she had seen the saints walking through Walgreens that day. I wanted to ask if she knew that this place was holy ground.

Pray for Us

The Catholic Church has an official Litany of the Saints, in which names of various saints are called out and following each name the response given by the people is "pray for us." It begins with invoking the names of God and Christ and then moving onto some of the names of Mary and the archangels before a long list of saints such as biblical saints, martyrs, and doctors of the church, and then familiar saints like Anthony, Benedict, Clare, and Catherine, all with the call to them to pray for us.

The Hebrew and Christian scriptures reveal a face of the Divine, who wants to create a new community unlike normal human societies. This community joins together heaven and earth, our human community with the Communion of Saints. I would add here that it draws together the community of creation as well. This is a communion of love. Through this community we support one another in many ways, but especially in our prayers, which are an act of witnessing and lifting one another up.

The book of Revelation reveals through an image of angels and saints who are already in heaven those who have passed across the threshold of life and death. This blessed community is engaged in the perpetual act of prayer for the human realm. It is through our sacred friendship with the angels and saints that they continue to stand at the altar and offer these prayers for our well-being, for our transformation, and ultimately to see ourselves as knit together in this sacred communion.

The Romans did not understand Christian devotion to saints and their relics. The early Christians worshipped in cemeteries and catacombs, among the holy dead. This was rooted in a belief in resurrection and new life to come. A belief that death is not the final word and we can connect through the veil with those who have left earthly life and still feel their steadfast support.

When we pray for someone, we move beyond our own narrow world and cares. We say through our prayers that the well-being of others, both human and the more-than-human world, matter. Prayer is a beautiful way to bring our love more fully into the world by honoring the struggles of others and standing with them in solidarity. Prayer means we widen our horizons of understanding and experience. We labor together to build the beautiful community we long for.

When we ask the saints to pray for us, we honor what they are already at work doing. They are standing in love, sending love, and invoking love. It helps to bind us together.

RELICS AND INCARNATION

Theologian Peter Brown, in his book *The Cult of the Saints*, describes his book as being about "the joining of Heaven and Earth, and the role, in this joining, of dead human beings."[1] He says the full implications of what this means have not been fully explored previously. By the end of the sixth century, graves of saints were in cemeteries outside of city walls. These became centers of church life. "This was because the saint in Heaven was believed to be 'present' at his tomb on earth."[2] Brown gives the example of an inscription on the grave of St. Martin of Tours, which reads, "Here lies Martin the bishop, of holy memory, whose soul is in the hand of God; but he is fully here, present and made plain in miracles of every kind."[3]

The dead were seen as active participants in the life of the living. The bones of the holy dead and other artifacts and bits of clothing would be brought into the city walls, breaching the previous divide between death and life. It was a holy person's human, earthly existence that led the living to believe that when the holy person died they continued in friendship with the community. This friendship could manifest as praying for them, protecting them, and intervening for them in other forms.

The saint's tomb was considered to be public property for those who identified as Christians; "it was made accessible to all and became the focus of forms of ritual common to the whole community."[4] Art and architecture were used to elevate their graves above those of the ordinary cemetery dwellers. A deep sense of reverence developed for these places. Miracles became associated with the tombs that "made visible the invisible refreshment of the saints; they are the early-Christian imagery of Paradise in action."[5] Music was played here, and the air was perfumed to reinforce this image.

Theodoret, a fifth-century bishop of Cyrrhus, described the connection people felt to the saints and martyrs as "intimate friends" and "invisible friends."[6] It was at this time that more and more Christian followers turned toward the dead for companionship, guidance, and protection. These invisible beings who had once been human maintained a living link.

Still later came the tradition of Christians taking on new names derived from the saints at Baptism, thereby deepening this link with the world of the dead and sense of their ongoing power and presence. A new identity was taken on, one rooted in a "new protecting spirit."[7]

Relics continue to be an important part of devotional life for some, as my opening story about the Ignatian relics I carried to our novena service demonstrates. At the end of each Mass of the Novena, dozens of people would line up in front of the two people assigned to hold the relics so they could be prayed over.

I had the privilege of holding the relics and praying over others several times, and even though the small metal box I held in my hand had just the tiniest chip of bone in it, it was incredibly moving to have person after person shuffle up to lean in toward me and whisper their prayer while touching the box. I would weep time and again as I listened to the burdens people carried. Sometimes there were prayers of gratitude for the gift of blessing too. But mostly the whispered prayers were of loss and heartache, and they included the sense that by stepping toward me and speaking their prayers aloud, they were entering into that communion shared between the living and the holy dead who love us and care for us. The physical bits of the saints carried forward through time are like a tether to their earthiness, their understanding of what it means to be human, and their desire to continue to pray for us in death as they did in life. The relics connect us to their embodiment of love. When they finished, I would offer a prayer that was meant to make them feel heard and to acknowledge our belief that God and the saints heard them too.

PRACTICE
Embodiment and Body Wisdom

Honoring relics feels like a profoundly embodied practice. This act of revering the physical remains of these holy ones who have passed through the veil is a way of still anchoring their lives in this earthly world. It is a way of saying that the saints know the struggles and joys of having a body, unlike the angels made purely of light.

Part of the practice of honoring intuitive ways of knowing and seeing involves tuning in more deeply to the messages our bodies give to us. Our bodies speak a language all their own, one that holds as much wisdom as our thinking and analyzing minds hold. My body regularly guides me in ways that my thoughts can't touch.

There are three doorways where we can begin if we are just starting to cultivate a connection to body wisdom. First is the breath, which is the animating force of our bodies. Breath is the gift of the Spirit that sustains us moment by moment. We can consciously slow our breath and bring more ease to our physical selves by activating our parasympathetic nervous system. One way to connect our breath more explicitly to prayer is to create a breath prayer, which can be repeated on each inhale and exhale. You might experiment with the following:

> *Inhale*: Breathing in, I am here.
> *Exhale*: Breathing out, I release.

This is a simple way to honor how breath can bring us more fully present and can also help us to soften and release physical tension we might be holding. Another gentle practice is to breathe slowly and imagine you are directing your breath to various parts of your body. As you do this, notice how each part feels and whether there is any holding or tightness in your body. Then see if you can allow your breath to soften this place in the body.

A final awareness we can find with the breath is when we consciously honor how our breathing is in a beautiful dance with the breathing of the plant world as we exchange oxygen and carbon dioxide. As we breathe in awareness of our communion with all of creation, we can also begin to imagine the saints breathing during their lifetimes. One of the inert gases we breathe is argon, which persists through generations, so we are literally breathing what our spiritual and generational ancestors breathed. We can hold this awareness when we breathe as well and deepen our communion across time.

The second way of deepening into our body wisdom is noticing body sensations. This is a more subtle awareness that grows over time. It is learning to notice how our bodies feel in response to various experiences and being able to glean that as wisdom our bodies offer to us. You may hear some people talk about a "felt sense" in their bodies or listening to their guts. Often when I am asked to make a decision about something, I sit with it for a period of time and notice how my body responds depending on which answer I give. We can ask the saints to help us strengthen our body connections in this way and even request that they speak to us through our body knowledge to guide us toward what is most life-giving.

The third way of developing a connection to our bodies is movement. This can be done with music or without. I recommend trying it both ways. Sometimes when we put on a piece of music, we might start to dance yet still not be fully present to how our bodies feel or respond in the moment. I invite you to try offering a prayer to a specific saint, but allow your body to lead your prayer. Give yourself maybe one minute at first. Spend a few moments breathing and dropping your awareness into your body. Then begin to listen to how your body longs to move and pray. This is not a linear prayer through words but a heartfelt and body-full prayer of our physical beings. This is a skill that can be developed over time just like learning any new language.

All three of these practices help us to root down into our embodied selves and listen to our hearts and the world through another kind of intelligence. It can help us to honor the wisdom of the Incarnation and how the holy dwells in us and among us.

MEDITATION
A Saint to Companion You

Begin by slowing down your breath and feeling your body present here now. Notice whether your body needs anything to feel more at ease, any gentle movement or stretching. Bring your breath to places of holding or tightness.

With intention, bring your awareness from your mind, the place of analyzing and anxiety, down to your heart center, where you can rest in the embrace of the Sacred Source of All. Allow a few moments to feel yourself held by the One who knit you into being, who birthed your soul into the world.

Call on the four archangels of Michael, Gabriel, Uriel, and Raphael to be with you in the four directions, creating a circle of light protecting you from any forces that wish you harm. Invite your guardian angel to be present beside you, holding any heaviness in your heart.

Then invite the Communion of Saints to gather around you as well, adding to that circle of light and protection already created so that there is now a powerful radiance shining from every direction.

Close your eyes for a moment if you are comfortable and see your life right now and the deep prayers of your heart. What are the choices you are being asked to make? How are you discerning what to say yes to and what to say no to? What is it that is being asked to be released? Rest here for a few moments in these desires and longings you hold for this season.

Add to that a prayer for a particular companion saint or patron saint for this season of your life. Remember that saints are those who have lived a life of love and compassion and aren't restricted by dogma or institution or even to a human body, as Thomas Merton so wisely tells us.

Hold your heart open to who your companion or patron saint for this time might be. See yourself encircled with the Divine, the angels, and the saints, and see one of the saints walking toward you with a wide smile and open arms. Notice who they are and how they appear to you. Is it someone you recognize or not? Ask them their name, and see what they reply.

Sit together for a while in the center of those circles of light. The saint tells you they are here to be a close companion for you in this next season. Share with this saint what is happening in your life right now: what feels heavy and what feels light, what you want to release and what you want to embrace more of. Then listen as they share the wisdom they have to offer you about how to be with all of these happenings and how to respond.

After they have offered their wisdom, sit together in the silence while you allow their words to wrap themselves around you and weave their way into your thoughts.

Make a commitment in the coming days to deepen your relationship with this particular saint by showing up in prayer and calling their name. Ask them what kind of ritual offering they desire from you to move into deeper connection and intimacy. Are there certain herbs or foods they love, certain ritual actions such as incense or candle lighting or offering a blessing, that you can offer to develop your relationship? Listen as they share what they would love from you.

Commit to those things you can say a full yes to and then offer an expression of your gratitude for this new or renewed friendship.

Deepen your breath again and slowly bring your awareness back to the room you are in. Write in a journal anything you want to remember from this time and any commitments you have made.

CREATIVE EXPLORATION
Write a Poem of Wisdom from a Saint to You

I love drawing on the saints as a subject of poetry. Think about an area
of your life you would like to have some advice, guidance, or wisdom
about. You could make it something significant, such as a calling, a
vocation, or a creative practice, or something less weighty, such as
maybe how to cook the best soup or knit a sweater. Then invite one
of the saints to be your companion and guide. It helps if you already
have a connection to who they are and some of the wisdom they bring
to the world, but searching online can augment your knowledge. Then
do some freewriting and have a conversation about your chosen topic
and see what emerges.

I include a poem I wrote here, titled "St. Hildegard Gives Her
Writing Advice," which looks to St. Hildegard of Bingen for advice on
how to be a writer.

Cry out and write,
were the words you heard
tumble toward you from
the blue-spattered sky
midway through your life,

Follow the greening,
you tell me in dreams
and I reach for the thread
which slips from my
close-clutched hand
on fine days.

How? I plead,
you show me my dog
playing in the sunlight,
the way shadows sashay
across my desk, and the orchid
holds out her purple tongue.

Always make time for tea,
you utter as you take me

by the hand through the garden,
show me dandelion and thistle,
yarrow and sage, *sipping*
slows you down so you can see.

Listen to the flowers teach,
you whisper,
find a meadow, lie down,
and wait for the poem to arrive,
I scoff and sigh
then find myself

among marigold, long
grasses, and loosestrife
all singing their glee
and my page is full
before I remember how
I resisted coming here at all.[8]

Blessing of the Saints

May the Communion of Saints
shower you with blessings,
may you seek their guidance
in moments of illness, confusion, gratitude.
We remember their own struggles,
living their humanity, enfleshed and tender.
We ask those across the threshold to pray for us,
knowing what it is to be wounded.
Call on the canonized saints,
Benedict, Francis, Ignatius,
Hildegard, Oscar Romero,
and the saints of spirit,
Howard Thurman, Dorothy Day, Thea Bowman,
and thousands of others
who witnessed to another way of being,

who helped to build a community of love.
Let them tether us to their earthiness
and remind us of the holiness
of bone and blood, the grace of our bodies
in bringing love to the world
and the presence of heaven here and now.
Feel them stretching themselves
back across the veil toward us,
in sacred friendship,
eyes shining, hearts radiant,
wisdom pouring like rainfall
after months of drought,
coming with a reminder
that you are never alone,
never forsaken,
and you dance in those life-giving
showers, celebrate Love as a visible
and invisible force, animating the world.

6

SAINTS AND PILGRIMAGE

To journey without being changed is to be a nomad.
To change without journeying is to be a chameleon.
To journey and be transformed by the journey is to be
a pilgrim.

—Mark Nepo

Pilgrimage is an ancient and embodied way to connect more intimately with the saints who inspire us. It is also a way to experience how a particular place shaped a saint's vision of the world and how the place itself still holds the memory and stories of particular people who lived vibrantly in those places. One of the ways we can do this is to go on an intentional sacred journey, a pilgrimage.

I fell in love with Hildegard of Bingen more than twenty years ago while studying her in graduate school. She quickly became an inspiring and wise companion to me as well as a mentor across time in the contemplative and creative life. Hildegard's principle of *viriditas*, or the greening power of God, became an essential life principle for me in discernment, as through her guidance, I now listen to where my life feels verdant and fertile and where it feels dry and barren.

She writes that this greening power of God is present in all creation:

> I flame above the beauty of the fields and I shine in the waters
> and I burn in the sun, the moon, and the stars. And with the
> airy wind I quicken all things with some invisible life, that
> sustains them all. For the air lives in viridity and in the flow-
> ers, the waters flow as if alive. . . . Therefore I, the fiery force,
> lie hidden in these things, and they burn because of me, just
> as breath continually moves a human being and a flickering
> flame exists within the fire. All of these things live in their
> essences and are not found in death, because I am life.[1]

Her mystical vision was to see the aliveness of all of creation and to see
how the sacred greening was the source and sustainer of all life.

I have gone on a personal pilgrimage to the Rhine Valley in
Germany, a place that deeply nourished her visions and work. I have
also had the privilege of bringing several groups of pilgrims to walk
gently and reverently on the pathways where Hildegard walked.

Standing in her shimmering landscape, *viriditas* came alive to me
in an even deeper way. I imagined her looking over the lush forests and
rivers and her own moment of first recognition that this outer vision
reflected an inner reality as well.

For Hildegard, the greenness of creation, which is an outward sign
of God's vitality at work in the world, is also a call to cultivate our inner
greening. The life that suffuses the world flows forth freely from the
life-creating and sustaining power of God, who is the primordial source
of greenness, connecting all living things to one another.

The "greening" of the area where she lived is powerful. She was a
landscape mystic, meaning that the geography of her world was a means
of ongoing revelation for her into the nature of God. Gazing out over
the shimmering autumn gold of the vineyards beyond St. Hildegard's
monastery in Rüdesheim, Germany, I felt this sense of deep surrender
where that porous line between myself and the earth seemed to fade.
I let that green energy of the earth rise up and embrace me in ways I
hadn't previously experienced. I imagined Hildegard breathing this
vision in and out. I felt God's creative power pulse through me in new
ways. The sacred is the quickening force animating and enlivening the

whole world, including our own beings. The flourishing of the world around Hildegard was an essential impetus for her to embrace her inner flourishing, and through her wisdom, it has become essential for my inner flourishing as well.

We can study her words, sing her music, gaze on her illuminated visions, and enter into her world through many portals. But to immerse ourselves in the physical landscape that shaped this creative outpouring is to take seriously the foundational impact the earth had on how she experienced life and the Divine Source of all that sustains us.

LEADING PILGRIMAGES

Soon after John and I moved to Galway, Ireland, in 2012, we began to discover many beautiful sacred sites nearby. Anyone local who heard about the spiritual work we did would suggest another place we should see. It turns out Ireland is saturated with the stone remains of Christian and pre-Christian holy places. There are dozens of these sites within an hour's drive of where we live and hundreds across Ireland.

With our own background in leading retreats and our love of pilgrimage as a sacred practice, we decided to try offering a pilgrimage in Ireland and see what kind of response we got. We were delighted that the first set of dates filled in a day. The second set of dates filled in a week. We ended up offering four different pilgrimage dates that first year.

We decided to structure them in a way that the pilgrimages would be a trip we would love to participate in, so our focus was on keeping them slow-paced, which meant visiting only one site a day, sometimes two. Even though we planned them to be slow, the more we led these programs, the more we found ourselves stripping down the excess so pilgrims could have spaciousness and time to really dwell at these sacred places. We didn't want them to be mere tourist stops where the bus halts for ten minutes and everyone piles off to take quick photos for their social media before rushing back onto the bus to the next thing. There really is very little possibility of having a genuine sacred and transformative encounter with a place in this rushed way that focuses on checking as much off a list as possible instead of allowing time and space to listen, savor, and discover.

Our other imperative was not moving from hotel to hotel each night but rather staying in Galway city the whole week in one bed-and-breakfast where the pilgrims could settle in and get to know the place over time. While someone walking the Camino, for example, might be moving from bed to bed each night—and there is certainly a place for this rhythm of pilgrimage, which has a different experience in mind—we wanted to invite our pilgrims to deepen into their relationship with where they were staying. What pilgrims told us repeatedly was that they felt they got a much deeper experience of Ireland by staying in one place and visiting far fewer sites than they ever did on previous whirlwind bus tours that circled Ireland in a week or two.

We brought our participants to pilgrimage pathways where we know pilgrims have walked for centuries. Ireland has been a site for various pilgrimages for hundreds of years, and the ancient monastic practice of hospitality would have been very much alive during those early centuries. Ireland was known as "the Land of Saints and Scholars" and has hundreds of recognized saints from this early medieval period. Each holy well is dedicated to a particular saint; the churches still carry the names of the men or women who founded them. It was the charism and holiness of the particular founder of each church or holy well that sparked the journeys that followed, both more than a thousand years ago and today.

Most of the sacred sites we brought our pilgrims to visit are what we might call "ruins." They are roofless stone churches open to the elements, allowing wind and sun and rain to become an integral part of our worship and prayer together in those spaces. Some of the holy wells are overgrown with wild herbs around them. Some of the stone crosses or round towers have been partially knocked down by time or the vandalism of Oliver Cromwell's forces and the history of British imperialism. But remarkably, many of the sites survived despite this destruction, and they still pulse with a sense of sacredness. The presence of the saints who founded these places is alive. You can feel the longings being held by the stones; you can imagine the others who have bowed down before the holy waters and dipped their hands in the refreshment of the well as they sought healing. You tie your ribbon onto the hawthorn tree and see the many dozens of other ribbons fluttering there, each a prayer.

We are extraordinarily grateful to all of the pilgrims who trusted us with their sacred voyages. We learned much from the experience, especially how to carefully create safe containers to hold the journey so that each person could step across the threshold that pilgrimage beckons us onto. It is a space of release of the old and awaiting the new, and it therefore is a vulnerable place. It is in the strangeness of the experience—unfamiliar places, language, and customs—that our hold on what is most familiar and on our entrenched patterns begin to soften. It is here that transformation has the space to happen.

The other essential aspect of these journeys was to have companions along the way. Community was always quickly created perhaps because of this sense of shared vulnerability and all being on a threshold of one kind or another. What the pilgrims shared along the way and at the end of each day's exploration always held gifts for the others in the group. Even if we go on pilgrimage alone, we will eventually need to share the experience with a soul friend to help us break it open more fully and bring those gifts back to the community.

PRACTICE
Making a Pilgrimage

If you are unable to travel due to limited resources or time, health, or global circumstances, you can make a pilgrimage by committing to a period of time—a few days is enough—to show up each day and pray with the words of the saint and mystic who stirs your heart. Commit to showing up each morning for a period of time; if you can only manage ten minutes, then let that be enough. If you can allow more spaciousness and sit for a half hour, that will gift you too. You can look for words of the mystic online or dip into a book with their words to reflect on and pray with.

There are many ways to practice pilgrimage. You can journey far away to a sacred site, but there are also options within reach of a walk or drive from home or even within your own imagination. Keep in mind these three essential aspects to create your own pilgrimage experience:

1. Begin with an intention and prayer or blessing for this time.
2. Stay open to the ways God might break in through the unexpected.
3. When you return, spend time reflecting on how this experience has touched you. What new discoveries or invitations did you hear?

Walking is a wonderful way to get out of our heads and into our bodies. If mobility issues prevent this, know that imagining yourself walking to each suggested site can have the same impact. God is present to us in whatever ways we are able to receive the sacred.

If you are physically able, make time to walk in your own neighborhood in a practice I call contemplative walking. These are walks in which you aren't trying to get to a destination; you aren't trying to increase your number of steps or monitor your heart rate. The purpose is to show up in the world and pay attention. Let your senses come alive. Drawing on the practice of intuitive consciousness from Chapter 2, pay attention to signs and symbols. Nature has a powerful way of communicating messages to us from the world beyond the veil. Ask whichever saint is calling to you to be present as you walk. Ask them to gift you with a symbol that might reveal some wisdom for your life direction. Then see what arrives in your path as you go.

Pilgrims also open themselves to being disoriented and to having their plans disrupted. If something happens along the way that wasn't "supposed" to in your preconceived ideas of how things would unfold, pause and see if there is a hidden gift here. Does this disruption move you out of your habitual ways of seeing and being?

Make a Local Pilgrimage

Chances are you live near a church or perhaps even several churches. You could choose to make a pilgrimage to your local cathedral. Using the three essential aspects, make it a sacred experience by blessing the journey there, paying attention for divine whispers along the way, and then reflecting when you return home. You might look up the Church calendar to see if there is an upcoming feast day that feels especially appropriate for your journey and let that shape your prayer.

In a more urban area, plan a walking pilgrimage from one church to another. Research the churches and map out a route. Look up the various saints they are dedicated to and write a note for each of them. Offer a prayer to each saint as you make each stop. Spend fifteen minutes in silence at each of the churches. Listen for what is offered to you. Remember that what can feel like interruptions or disruptions to your plans may contain the sparks of an encounter with the Divine.

If you live in a rural area, still try this suggestion, but you may need to drive between sites. Try keeping the car radio off to maintain an atmosphere of quiet reflection.

Begin your pilgrimage by reading of the disciples meeting Jesus on the road to Emmaus (Lk 24:13–35) as a blessing for this time. Listen along the way for how the holy is being revealed to you.

Make a Nature Pilgrimage

You might choose to make a pilgrimage to a nearby place in nature. This could be a local park that you love or even your backyard. You could locate the closest forest, river, seashore, or mountain, remembering as you do all of the holy landscapes in scripture, such as the Jordan River, the Sea of Galilee, Mount Horeb, or Mount Sinai. Or you might want to use this nature pilgrimage as a way to connect to one of the creation-centered mystics, such as Francis of Assisi.

Begin your pilgrimage by reading Psalm 104 and asking for the clarity to hear all of creation joining in an ongoing hymn of praise. As you walk, let this be a time of contemplative listening for the more-than-human voices that surround you. Spend time with things that call to you along the way, whether a pinecone in your path, a smooth stone, moss on the trees, or a flower growing. Pay attention to the birds and animals that make this place their home, and call to mind the desert and Celtic saints who saw intimacy with animals as a special sign of holiness. Find a quiet place on your journey to sit for a time in silence and simply receive the gifts being offered to you.

Peregrinatio

The ancient Irish monks and mystics had a very unique approach to pilgrimage. They would set out on a journey for Christ, often by boat without oar or rudder, and let the currents of divine love carry them to the place of their resurrection. This is the place where their gifts and the needs of the community came together and they were able to serve fruitfully. This type of pilgrimage was known as a *peregrinatio.*

Instead of a literal journey by boat, you can work with the spirit of this pilgrimage experience by going for a contemplative walk without destination. Begin your pilgrimage by reading the story of Abraham and Sarah being called to leave their homeland in search of a new country (Gn 12:1–2). Bless this time and release any desire for a goal or outcome. Take some deep breaths to center yourself, and then see where your feet take you. You aren't trying to get anywhere; the goal is simply to be present moment by moment to the call of the Spirit. See where your attention is drawn, pause often, and linger. Call on a favorite saint to be with you.

Cultivating this as a regular practice helps us to open up to *peregrinatio* in our daily lives when we are called to release our grasp on the life we think we need and instead be open to the sacred possibilities being offered to us.

MEDITATION
Pilgrimage of the Imagination

Choose a particular saint you'd like to make a pilgrimage to in your imagination. You might choose one of the European mystics such as Hildegard of Bingen or Teresa of Avila. It might be an African mystic such as Desmond Tutu or Augustine of Hippo or the Desert Mothers and Fathers. Perhaps you are drawn to a more contemporary mystic from North America such as Howard Thurman or Dorothy Day.

To engage in this meditation, you will first need to do a little bit of research. Search online for some articles about the saint you want to encounter. In particular, make note of where they lived or journeyed to.

Then search online for images of these places by entering the place name in the search bar and clicking the image tab. Select four to five images that especially spark your imagination or some kind of longing. You can print these out, or you can keep them bookmarked in your browser or saved to your photo album on your device.

Look online and find images of the places your favorite saint lived and imagine yourself there. The imagination is a powerful portal and can transport us across time and space. We can close our eyes and see ourselves wandering those pathways, embraced by that landscape, and breathe it all in to see what it speaks to our own soul. We can see ourselves coming to meet our saint or mystic as we draw closer to them in the places where they lived, worked, and loved.

CREATIVE EXPLORATION
Write a Prayer for the Pilgrim Journey

Spend some time connecting to your inner longing for pilgrimage and journeying to the land of the saint and mystic who calls to your heart. Listen for the prayer arising. If you are feeling called to the pilgrim experience, what is it about that voyage that sparks your imagination? Perhaps you are standing at a crossroads in your life and are discerning a new pathway. Maybe you are experiencing the loss of a loved one, a dream, a job, or an ability and need time to grieve and integrate.

Listen for the words and images that arise in the quiet and make room for them on the page. Don't worry about making a coherent prayer at first; simply allow whatever is stirring in you to have some space to be received. Once you feel you have gotten in touch with the deep desires of your heart, turn your attention to writing the prayer. Begin by calling on the saint you want to encounter, from whom you are seeking support. Follow with your supplication.

Then hold this prayer lightly. It is important to name your longings, and it is also important to make room for whatever inspiration that comes. Perhaps part of your prayer could be to hold everything lightly and be open to the new possibilities that emerge in this experience.

Blessing the Journey

May you see all of life as a pilgrimage,
walking a sacred path toward intimacy
with all the invisible ones
who journey alongside us.
Ask that your steps each be blessed
with guidance and humility,
that you release the need to know
where you are headed
and trust the path itself.
May you be blessed with an open heart
to receive the stranger along the way
as well as deep within.
Call on the great communion of pilgrims
throughout time who wandered
for love of the great Journeyer.
Remember Jesus who walked dusty roads
healing others and feasting with outcasts,
the Desert Mothers and Fathers
traveling to wild solitary places
for radical communion with God.
Remember Francis and Ignatius
journeying to Rome for study and guidance,
Teresa setting up her monasteries,
Hildegard preaching Sophia's wisdom,
the Celtic monks seeking to dwell on the edges,
making a sanctuary upon islands in the sea.
Know their impulse to seek a new horizon
as one that calls you onward as well.
Feel their love lightening your burden,

drawing you closer to the One
who shaped you, who shows you
you are always both in exile and at home,
who reminds you that love
is all you need to carry.

Part Three

ANCESTORS

7

BLESSINGS OF OUR ANCESTORS

Therefore, since we are surrounded by so great a
cloud of witnesses, let us also lay aside every weight
and the sin that clings so closely, and let us run with
perseverance the race that is set before us.

—Hebrews 12:1

In the introduction I mentioned some foundational assumptions about the work of this book, which focuses on our relationship with those who dwell in the invisible world. These include a belief that we can have a relationship with the angels, saints, and ancestors and that they desire that as well.

Most religious traditions—such as Christianity, Judaism, Islam, Hinduism, Buddhism, and many Indigenous traditions—have some kind of teaching and practice of conscious relationship with ancestors.

When engaging with the ancestors, I believe along with the teaching of the Christian tradition that

- there is some kind of consciousness or awareness that continues beyond death in this world;

- we can be in relationship with the ancestors;
- not all of the dead are fully well (unlike the saints we explored, some ancestors will die in a state of deep unresolved trauma and wounding that is then passed down their generational line); and
- the dead can change and be affected by our actions, and the reverse is true as well, we are impacted by them too.[1]

We will explore in these remaining chapters various ways to cultivate a relationship with the ancestors. You can do this even if you know nothing about your bloodline. St. Paul writes in his letter to the Hebrews about the great cloud of witnesses (Heb 12:1–2). They are the ones who inspire us to endure through life's challenges and find joy, cultivate love, and discover purpose to our days.

There are two main parts to this work. One is to connect with those ancestors who are wise and well and seek their support for our own lives. The second part of the work is to bring healing to the ancestors who are not fully well and working in various ways to bring healing to the family line.[2] We will work with healing more in the next chapter.

Sandra Easter, a Jungian analyst and author of *Jung and the Ancestors*, describes the process this way: "Coming into a more conscious relationship with the ancestors is a home coming, a return to origins, to a way of knowing, seeing, and being in relationship with the world that has been and is part of our collective inheritance."[3] She says that this is what psychologist Carl Jung would have described as "archaic" knowing, drawing on our ancient roots from those for whom connecting to the ancestors would have been a natural and expected part of daily living.

In her book *This Here Flesh*, Cole Arthur Riley writes, "I believe in a spiritual realm that is so enmeshed with the physical that it is imperceptible. I believe in the mysterious nearness of my ancestors, but I believe they are located at the site of my own blood and bone."[4] The ancestors are already with us. Calling upon them simply opens our awareness to their presence. Prayer and ritual mean developing a relationship with them and listening for their wisdom in our lives.

Thresholds

In Celtic tradition there are many moments considered to be a "thin time," which means that heaven and earth feel closer and we might experience moments of connection to those who have gone before us in ways that we don't usually.

These moments include the daily portals of dawn and dusk as the world moves from dark to light and back to dark again. They also include the eight threshold moments of the year, which are the solstices, the equinoxes, and the cross-quarter days that fall between the solstices and equinoxes. Of these eight, Samhain, which falls on November 1, is considered to be the thinnest time, when the ancestors and spirits walk among us. The door between the spiritual and the physical is even further open than at other times. Samhain is the start of the dark half of the year. It is the season of rest, incubation, and mystery. It is the season of dreamtime and the perfect time of year to open your heart to connect with those who journeyed before you. Winter invites us to gather inside, grow still with the landscape, and listen for the voices we may not hear during other times of the year. These may be the sounds of our own inner wisdom or the voices of those who came before us. Listen for the messages of the ancestors in those days especially—they will speak their wisdom through raven and stone, tree and rain, dreams and synchronicities. This is the language through which we receive these gifts and only need to open ourselves to them.

The Celtic feast of Samhain coincides with the Christian celebration of All Saints' Day on November 1 and All Souls' Day on November 2, which begin a whole month in honor of those who have died. We tend to neglect our ancestral heritage in our Western culture, but in other cultures, remembering the ancestors is an intuitive and essential way of beginning anything new. We don't recognize the tremendous wisdom we can draw on from those who have traveled the journey before us and whose DNA we carry in every fiber of our bodies.

Prayer and Ritual

Consider spending some time each morning opening your senses to all
the ways you might experience a connection to your ancestors. Keep a
journal by your bed and pay attention to your dreams. We may receive
a message while we sleep or be offered a symbol to help connect to
us. Notice the synchronicities of everyday life—those moments of
meaningful coincidences—and keep track of them as well. We can easily
dismiss a subtle moment of connection to a loved one who has passed on
or to the wider body of ancestors. If a song starts playing, you encounter
a meaningful symbol, or someone says something to you that brings a
sense of deeper knowing, start trusting these as moments of connection.
The more we dismiss them, the fainter the connection becomes. The
more we cultivate an honoring of these kinds of experiences, the more
we notice them happening. Often when a synchronicity happens we will
feel a kind of tingling sensation or chill and we will sense something
magical or otherworldly is happening. When this happens, pause and
receive. Notice when your mind wants to undermine what happened.

Spend significant time in nature and listen for the wisdom of trees
and animals. I have often had experiences of encounter with each of
my parents in creation. From coyotes to butterflies, cuckoo birds to
rainbows, these moments gave me a sense of deep connection.

Theologian Patrick Reyes describes intuition as "the expression of
guides and spirits. In many ways, the wisdom and spirit of my ancestors
live in my very bones. The sum of my experiences, to borrow from
[adrienne maree brown] makes up my intuition. . . . To cultivate your
intuition, *slow down*."[5] He goes on to write about his grandmother who
witnessed to this way of being for him: "It was in her ability to slow us
down and draw on the deep ancestral wisdom she carried in her very
body. Intuition is not another form of problem solving. It draws on the
love that threads its way through generations."[6]

Ritual has a way of bridging the gap between the visible and
invisible worlds and between the conscious and unconscious knowing.
We can open ourselves to communication from our grandmothers and
grandfathers. What we work on consciously through ritual and prayer

has an impact in the world of the ancestors. Ritual is the intentional cultivation of relationship, but communication happens in spontaneous ways as well.

Engage the arts, movement, and poetry in service to this quest because they speak the intuitive language. We are not concerned with making beautiful things, only authentic expressions of the stirrings of the soul; in the process, beauty will emerge in its own form. We are calling upon the love that is our inheritance and makes itself available to us through intuitive connection to those who came before us. The arts are a way we can feel our way forward, tending to the unique shape of our ancestral wisdom. These are all places where the Otherworld breaks through and speaks to us.

Dr. Barbara Holmes reminds us that it is not the ritual or practice that ensures we are visited by the Divine: "Human receptivity and presence merely ensure openness to this possibility. It is the turning toward mystery; the readiness to receive that prepares the way for spiritual engagement."[7] We do not do this work ourselves. But we do prepare ourselves in openness and readiness to have an encounter with the Holy One and the love of thousands.

We can begin a relationship with our ancestors by creating an altar in our home (there is an invitation to do this at the end of the chapter) and inviting in their presence to our daily prayer. Bringing the ancestors directly into our prayer and ritual is a way to lovingly grow in our connections with them.

Pastor and social activist Vincent Harding writes, "The voice (of the ancestors) has entered so profoundly into me that I am flesh of their flesh, bone of their bone, song of their song, pain of their pain, hope of their hope."[8] He goes on to describe hearing the voices of his children, "I believe that ancient rivers of our people flow in them. I hear their voices, and I know what it means. It means I am called to be father, rock, and strength, encourager for the struggles of tomorrow, baptizer in the rivers of their past."[9] The ancestors pulse in our blood and bone. Their ancient voices echo in our hearts.

In Christian ritual and liturgy, there is the celebration on the Feasts of All Saints and All Souls. Some churches keep a Book of the Dead,

in which the names of loved ones who died are written and kept near
the altar so they may be remembered at Masses throughout November.
November is the month of the dead, and churches often have special
Masses of remembrance throughout the month as well as setting up a
special ancestral altar somewhere in the church space where members
can bring photos, flowers, and other offerings. Many churches also
have votive candles available all year, which people can light either as
a prayer for themselves or another or in remembrance of a loved one.

In medieval Europe, there were many practices for All Souls' Day,
including creating altars, celebrating requiem Masses, lighting candles
and bonfires, visiting graves, ringing bells, and making soul cakes,
which were small, round, spiced loaves to commemorate the dead that
were given out to people who came door to door.

The Office of the Dead

The Office of the Dead is part of the Liturgy of the Hours in the
Catholic, Anglican, and Lutheran churches.[10] It is a prayer cycle on
behalf of those who have died that is always said on the Feast of All
Souls (November 2) but is also said at other times of year—either alone
or in community—when a loved one passes away. It is composed of
various psalms, scriptures, and other readings.

These prayers are offered both as an act of loving remembrance for
those who have died and as an act to help them enter more fully into
the Divine Presence. Praying for the dead is a prayer of intercession.
Rooted in the assumption that not all dead are fully well when they
pass through the veil, part of this Office is to pray on their behalf for
full healing. The Catholic Church calls this time of purification after
death *purgatory* (which is different than teachings on hell), a time that
allows the dead to become fully well so they can enter into the fullness
of joy of the heavenly realm. The Church also teaches that fasting,
giving money to the poor, and works of penance can be offered up on
behalf of the dead. St. John Chrysostom, one of the early church fathers,
wrote, "Let us not hesitate to help those who have died and to offer our

prayers for them" (Homilies on 1 Corinthians 41:5; cf. Job 1:5). We will be exploring more healing of our ancestral lineages in the next chapter.

Día de los Muertos

In Mexico, Day of the Dead celebrations called Día de los Muertos thrive. There are many practices that are part of these celebrations, including creating an *ofrenda*, which is a temporary family altar with photos of loved ones. Decorations include sugar skulls, which are reminders of our mortality and the passing from flesh into spirit, and marigolds, which remind us of the beauty of the life that endures beyond the veil. Those celebrating this time will leave out bread and drink for the dead who visit in the night. Families celebrate with a picnic in the graveyard, sharing stories of their ancestors, singing songs, and praying the Rosary.

In the Aztec culture that preceded modern Mexican culture, there was a belief in two deaths: the first when the person physically dies and the second when the person is forgotten.[11] These rituals around remembering the dead and inviting their spirits to be present among the living was a way to delay this second death.

Jewish Practices

When someone Jewish dies, their community gathers together to recite the Mourner's Kaddish regularly in the year following their death and, in the years that follow, on the anniversary of their death. It is not a prayer of mourning or grief but a prayer of praising the Divine on their behalf. Five times during the year, on specific holidays, Jews say Yizkor, which is a memorial liturgy for all who have died.

Another Jewish practice is honoring *yahrzeit*, which means "year time" in Yiddish and refers to the annual anniversary of the death of a loved one. These are mainly marked in community by reciting the Kaddish and with good acts, as well as lighting the yahrzeit candle, which is a candle of remembrance. It is lit at sundown the night before the anniversary and remains lit until it burns out the following day after sunset.

We find in the Hebrew Scriptures the practices of stones used as markers on graves to remember where a body has been buried. Jews still bring stones to cemeteries and place these stones on the graves as an act of remembrance and connection.

OTHER TRADITIONS

Malidoma Somé, born into a Dagara community in West Africa, says that in this worldview, "death is not a separation but a different form of communion, a higher form of connectedness with the community, providing an opportunity for even greater service."[12] For the Dagara people, ancestors are intimately connected to the world of those living on this side of the veil. When someone dies, they continue to be part of the human community.

Gary Eberle, in his book *Sacred Time and the Search for Meaning*, writes about various cultural beliefs in the ancestral realm:

> The ancient Irish believed the souls of the dead went west over the great sea, a belief that must have made my Irish ancestors' departure for the New World more poignant. Many Native Americans believed in a land of the dead that is remarkably like the one the living inhabit. And in African tribes, the dead form an integral part of the life of the village and are regularly included in feasts and rites. The ancient Romans believed that their children were reincarnations of ancestors who had waited in the Elysian Fields until a suitable body was ready. All Souls' Day reminded me that what lives on from generation to generation.[13]

We have largely lost a sense of regular connection to our ancestors, especially those who died before we were even born. Like the saints, our wise and well ancestors can be a source of tremendous wisdom and support as we move through this life. And we can help bring healing to those who are not fully vibrant at death.

We communicate with ancestors much in the way we would communicate with angels and saints—through dreams, visions, synchronicity, nature, ritual, and imagination. We call upon them through prayer, we honor them through ritual offerings, and we ask them for guidance.

Henri Nouwen offers us this wisdom:

> As we grow older we have more and more people to remember, people who have died before us. It is very important to remember those who have loved us and those we have loved. Remembering them means letting their spirits inspire us in our daily lives. They can become part of our spiritual communities and gently help us as we make decisions on our journeys. Parents, spouses, children, and friends can become true spiritual companions after they have died. Sometimes they can become even more intimate to us after death than when they were with us in life. Remembering the dead is choosing their ongoing companionship.[14]

I especially love that final sentence: "Remembering the dead is choosing their ongoing companionship." This is an intentional act of cultivating relationship.

For some of us, when we think about ancestors, our thoughts may immediately turn toward a dysfunctional family system or a legacy of pain and woundedness we carry in our family line. Perhaps you had a very toxic family system, and so the thought of naming blessings that have come from them seems ridiculous or too much of a stretch. Rest assured, we will be working on some ways to bring healing to our family lines. But first I want to invite us to ponder the blessing of our ancestors.

Perhaps you were adopted and never knew your birth family. It might help as well to consider our ancestors not just of blood and bone but also of spiritual lineage, creative lineage, or other vocational inspiration. Let us consider that our ancestors bless us in innumerable ways as well. We can get consumed by the healing work that needs to happen; indeed, it is a lifelong journey. In Somatic Experiencing,[15] a field of work to address trauma, the work begins with resourcing ourselves by connecting to something pleasurable. This can be a portal to grace. Similarly, we can begin with naming the blessings our ancestors have bestowed on us as a way of grounding ourselves in the gifts of our genetic and spiritual lines before tending to the wounds.

The first fundamental blessing we can offer gratitude for is the gift of life itself. No matter what kind of family we came from, no matter how much suffering was caused, there is the fundamental impulse toward life that we can celebrate. We can give thanks for being here, being fully alive, and even having the privilege of taking time to do this healing work: to explore spiritual practices and to ponder what makes our lives meaningful. Many of our ancestors never had that luxury. Many worked very long hours for little reward and were never able to pause and ask themselves how their own generational connection could bring more wisdom to their lives.

I like to remember as well that in the midst of my ancestors' struggles there was at least some resilience and courage developed that I have inherited. This is the second fundamental blessing we can offer gratitude for. I may never know what they went through exactly, but I can sometimes feel their sturdiness and how they endured. They too lived through times of war and plague and economic struggle.

Sometimes when I go outside at night and can see the brilliance of the stars, I remember that my ancestors also had moments of wonder and awe standing with their faces upturned toward the vast expanse of the universe. I remember that they too had moments of delight, of joy, of dancing, no matter how hard their lives were.

DNA AND GENEALOGICAL RESEARCH

The gospels of Matthew and Luke both present us with Jesus's genealogy. Matthew begins with Abraham, and Luke begins with Adam. The lists are identical between Abraham and David, but the rest of the ancestors vary widely. Ann Patrick Ware, in a book titled *Remembering the Women*, wrote the genealogy of women for Jesus.[16] The Christian gospels value this sense of lineage and where Jesus came from. We can take encouragement from them for our own search for our roots.

How do we begin to learn about our ancestry? DNA tests are a boon, especially for those who are either adopted or disconnected from their family story, as they can tell us the lands our ancestors dwelled upon and what landscapes and stories shaped them. It is a great way to start knowing more about the lands that shaped our ancestors. The percentages revealed by the tests of background do shift a bit over time as they do more research. None of them are one hundred percent accurate, but they certainly give you a good sense of what is true about your blood and bone and comprise a valuable doorway into connecting to your ancestors.

Even when you don't have access to these kinds of genealogical records, there are still ways to meet your ancestors. Sandra Easter writes that "having access to genealogical records and historical documents helped us place our personal stories in the context of our ancestors' stories. I have found that even when genealogical information isn't available, information about this dynamic is often presented in dreams and can be discovered in dialogues with the ancestors."[17] As she reminds us, there are many ways to enter into relationship with one's ancestors, even if we don't have access to specific details and facts.

Of course, if we do have some basic genealogical information of parents and perhaps grandparents, ancestry websites allow us to build our family trees and link to the trees of others so we can discover lines that were lost to us. I have found that working with genealogical researchers in the countries where I am seeking connections has also been invaluable. They can look up records in languages I do not speak and verify connections between various people in my family. Sometimes there are stories of hidden records. The census tells me about the kind of work an ancestor was engaged in. Death certificates tell stories about the illnesses or other causes that brought about their death.

VISITING CEMETERIES

When I lived in Seattle I went once to a cemetery north of the city to meet my friend and writing/teaching partner Betsey Beckman, who was doing some filming for a dance video she was creating.

I absolutely love cemeteries and am used to having strange and serendipitous encounters there. As we finished shooting, her videographer brought out some champagne to celebrate nearing the end of a wonderful project. We lay down in the grass under the golden light of the evening sky and relished the moment. Talking and laughing, I saw a man heading our way, and I worried we had been disturbing his peace at the cemetery. Instead, he walked up to us with his three-year-old daughter and offered us cupcakes to go with our champagne. Then his little girl started playing with the videographer's four-year-old son, romping and frolicking together among the gravestones with sheer delight.

We thanked our new friend for his generosity and asked him his story. His wife had died a year before of cancer, and he came there often to the cemetery to remember her and celebrate her life. For him, laughing, running, playing, and having cupcakes and champagne were just how you should act at the cemetery when remembering a woman filled with light and love. He told us of how this young mother, who knew she would die and not see her daughter grow up, wrote this young girl letters for every birthday she would have for the next several years, offering her loving advice.

Cemeteries are often associated with scary movies, ghouls, and zombies. But the cemetery, even if it isn't the place where your ancestors are buried, can be a place of beauty, stillness, and reflection. You might even consider bringing champagne and cupcakes and having a picnic to celebrate the ones who walked this earth before you. For all the hardships in their lives, there was also joy, joy that deserves to be celebrated.

PRACTICE
Blessing and Gratitude

Both the Jewish and Celtic Christian traditions have the beautiful practice of blessing. These blessings include blessings for the world as well as blessings for each and every encounter and experience, the most ordinary moment, the tasks of the day.

In this worldview, every single thing we encounter and each act we perform becomes worthy of blessing. Gratitude is offered for the gift of every moment—upon awakening, when crossing a threshold, while eating a meal, and when lighting candles. This act of blessing is really a special way of paying attention. It is mindfulness infused with gratitude. It is a moment of remembering wonder as our primary response to the world. It is an act of consecrating time.

In the Benedictine monastic tradition, everything is considered sacred. The stranger at the door is to be welcomed in as Christ. The kitchen utensils are to be treated with the same respect as the altar vessels. Perhaps most important for our practice, the hinges of the day call us to remember the presence of God again and again, so that time becomes a cascade of prayers. What if I move through the day, and each time I begin a new task, I pause and consecrate what I am about to do?

This practice of blessing our moments is a powerful one, and one that cultivates a sense of gratitude and abundance. Rather than think we are owed something or things should be a certain way, we recognize and honor that all of life is a gift.

We can begin to see all the everyday things of our lives as openings into the rich depths of the world: the steam rising from my coffee, the bird singing from a tree branch outside my window, the doorbell announcing a friend's arrival, and the meal that nourishes my body for service. Each of these moments invites us to pause and see it through a different kind of vision.

Then we can bring another dimension to this practice by bringing in an awareness of our ancestors. When I savor my tea, I might imagine my grandmother also enjoying a cup of peppermint brewed in quiet moments. When I eat something delicious, I might remember my grandfather's love of sweets and chocolate cake in particular. When I delight in the birds that sing the morning awake, I call to mind the bird feeder my grandparents had hanging outside the kitchen window and the moments of pausing to say *ahhh* and *ohhh, look how beautiful*. At events like birthday parties or weddings, I can see generations of family in my imagination singing and dancing.

These moments of blessing become an opportunity to give thanks for the grace in my life, the simple gifts that bring joy and meaning. They can be moments when I connect to the joy that swims in my blood and bone. I can offer gratitude for their moments of pleasure in the midst of how hard life can be. I can give thanks for my life each morning and remember that I am only here because of the love of thousands upon thousands over time. I can send blessings back through time to each of them, blessings of forgiveness, blessings of appreciation.

MEDITATION
Connecting to Wise and Well Ancestors

Begin by first brewing a cup of tea—any kind of tea you enjoy. Let yourself choose something that would feel deeply nourishing right now.

Let every moment of the brewing be sacred: boiling the water, choosing the tea to drink, pouring the water over, and watching as the tea slowly steeps into the water, that magic of heat and time. Bring your tea to your prayer space.

Notice any distractions around you, anything you could turn off or unplug, a door you could shut to let both yourself and others know you are creating a boundary around this time of prayer.

Continue by slowing your breath and letting it anchor you deeply into the ground beneath you. Feel your whole body begin to settle downward; imagine sending roots into the soil, feeling the rich nourishment of humus.

Drop your awareness into your heart center, seeing yourself in the cave of your heart and, within that cave, held by the ancient embrace of the Mother, the feminine form of the Divine who set all of creation into being. She is the primordial matrix of all creation, from whom all life emerged. Rest there with her, knowing there is nothing that needs to be done in this moment; you can simply rest into the gift of being, breathing, and beholding this moment.

Invite in the archangels, your guardian angel, the Communion of Saints, and your patron or companion saint for this season of your life. Ask them along with the Great Mother to create a sacred boundary of protection around you. See what color and intensity of light appears or any other form the sacred boundary takes.

As you sip your tea, imagine traveling back in time through many generations, perhaps hundreds of generations of men and women, your ancestors. Ask to be shown a wise and well ancestor from any of your lineages. When someone shows up, spend a few moments together and ask if they are wise and well, ask if they are your foremother or forefather, and check with your own body to see how it feels. If you don't feel well in your body with them, ask them to leave and then go on to the next person.

If you feel well in body with this connection, greet this ancestor and perhaps offer a cup of your tea to them. Invite them to speak about their lives, and see if you can tell where and when they come from. There is no need to force this; just notice if an awareness arises.

Sit for a while together in silence as well. Then ask for a blessing, and let your ancestor take your hands in theirs, your hands still warm from the tea. Your ancestor gestures in some way so you know something of their wisdom for you.

You offer your gratitude, and they ask you to return to visit sometime.

You deepen your breath and slowly and gently return to the room you are in. Write down anything you noticed or discovered.

CREATIVE EXPLORATION
Ancestors Altar and a Calendar of Feast Days

Much like our work with the angels and saints, you are now invited to create an altar for your ancestors. This could be a separate altar or one combined with the other two. You might look through old family photos if you have them, or if you have a symbol or memento that might be a talisman, place that on your altar to help remind you of your ancestors. You could focus on one or two beloved family members who have passed away, or you could focus on your ancestors in general as the great cloud of witnesses. Consider if you have anything passed down to you that would help anchor your awareness and memory. Candles are a beautiful symbol of the light that endures, and incense is a symbol of the way our prayers move back and forth across the veil.

Every year on October 19 I find a way to honor the memory of my own mother's death through ritual and being in the forest or by the sea. On this day, I have encountered a rainbow appearing in the sky, a coyote in the cemetery on a foggy morning, and a synchronicity through music that led me to be sure my mother was present with me.

One year on this anniversary I went to yoga class. I arrived early to have a few moments of silence to begin this sacred time of entering the body's wisdom. As I moved into the room, there was an ethereal woman's voice singing. Another student asked the teacher what music this was. "*Hymns to the Divine Mother*," she replied. I smiled and let the rise and fall of the music carry my breath. When class started, we began in child's pose and were invited to bring an intention for the class or to offer our practice on behalf of someone. I offered this time to my mother. Then we moved into our first pose, butterfly, and I began to gently weep. Butterflies were a significant symbol when my mother died. Sometimes the dead reach through the veil in unmistakable ways if we are attuned and paying attention. She was there with me in that space, and my whole practice became a joyful place of reaching across thresholds, inner and outer, here and beyond.

You can also go on a contemplative walk in nature and pay attention to any symbols that show up on your path. Leaves, feathers, or acorns can all be powerful reminders of those who walked before us: leaves for how they too are released from this world, feathers for the wings they travel on between worlds, and acorns as seeds of future generations.

You can then add dates to your calendar, such as the dates loved ones died. In many cultures and traditions, the anniversary of death is an important time of remembrance. Consider making time to celebrate the life of these ancestors in some way, perhaps serving their favorite food or visiting a landscape they loved. You could also add birthdays and wedding anniversaries if you want to get more complex. If you are researching your family tree on an ancestry website, you could decide to include the death dates of a certain number of generations in your calendar.

If you don't have any of this information from your ancestors, you can also choose to make November a sacred time of year for remembrance. On the Feasts of All Saints and All Souls (November 1 and 2, respectively), you might create or renew your ancestral altar and add fresh flowers and other offerings to it. Consider making a commitment to pray with and for your ancestors each day during the month.

The Blessings of Our Ancestors

This blessing calls you home again
to your collective inheritance of blood and bone,
calls you to dance with generations
who shimmer beyond the veil.
We call on the great cloud of witnesses,
the ones who inspire our courage,
support our endurance,
kindle our joy, whisper words of hope.
May the wise and well ones,
who are vibrant and radiant with healing,
who have stepped into the expanse of love
without hesitation, whose hearts are open wide,
shower you with their blessing
so you know your ancient inheritance.
Stand at a threshold
and whisper some of their names,
grandmothers and grandfathers,
back through hundreds and thousands of years,
prayers and supplications
for all that helps you navigate this world with ease.
May they form a circle of protection around you
to guard from anything that would wish you harm.
Open the eyes of your heart to see
they are already here, already dancing

through your feet, your hips, your hands,
the embrace of your arms,
the undulations of your spine, the smile on your lips.
This blessing dances in the threshold space with you,
at the turning of dawn or dusk,
helping your heart stay open, attuned,
to the wisdom pouring forth.
Sing aloud of gratitude, ask them to surround you,
knowing they are already present,
it is only your vision that must change to see.

8

INTERGENERATIONAL WOUNDS AND OUR RESPONSIBILITIES

The LORD is slow to anger and filled with unfailing love,
forgiving every kind of sin and rebellion. But he does
not excuse the guilty. He lays the sins of the parents
upon their children; the entire family is affected—even
children in the third and fourth generations.

—Numbers 14:18 (The New Living Translation)

Ancestral healing and connection work has been a significant part of my spiritual journey since about 2005. That was the time I walked into the office of a Jungian analyst to process the unabating grief I felt over my mother's death. He introduced me to family systems theory and to the ways Carl Jung believed we carry on the unresolved traumas of our ancestors. All these years later, he is still my spiritual director and I continue this work of connecting to my ancestors because it is a path that has brought me tremendous personal healing and a deeper connection to who I am called to be.[1]

When I imagine ancestral work, I see layers and layers of story, concentric rings or circles—my story is embedded in the story of my family, which is nestled in the story of my parents' families, and so on back through generations. For me, ancestral work started with being in conversation with my deceased and then, from there, examining the dysfunctional and toxic patterns of family relationships with parents, grandparents, aunts, uncles, and cousins. This genetic story is wrapped in cultural stories, the places and events that shaped the people who came before me—language, music, landscape, and even the trauma of war, which epigenetic evidence shows carries down from generation to generation. Within me is a sacred thread that ties me to everyone in my ancestral past. I carry within me the wounds and unfulfilled longings, the hopes and dreams, of everyone who came before me. Learning their stories means I come to know my own more intimately.

Our Western culture doesn't make much room for the honoring of ancestors or valuing what connection to the stories of our past might bring to us. When we uncover the layers of the stories we have lived for generations, though, we begin to understand ourselves better. Some of these stories we may know the details of, and some we may have to access and experience in an embodied and intuitive way. These memories live inside of us, waiting for us to give them room in our lives.

As we have already seen in our reflections on the saints, the Church teaches that the dead go on living in a different form, that the dead are not all equally well (indeed, the saints are celebrated for being especially well), and the dead and living can communicate with one another at the very least through the vessel of prayer and ritual.

These teachings are also some of the fundamental assumptions we make when we engage in ancestral healing work. Other core beliefs are that we can have a relationship with the dead, and the dead can change even after passing through the veil. I have found both of these beliefs to be profoundly true. Even if we might think of the Catholic Church teaching about purgatory as outdated, I think many of us can agree that some people who die are not as deeply aligned in love and freedom as others.

The African ritualist Malidoma Somé writes, "It is the responsibility of the living to heal their ancestors."[2] In many Indigenous cultures, there is a much more active and ongoing engagement with the ancestors. Author James Baldwin describes the difference between birthright and inheritance as well as how we are given both by our ancestors: "My inheritance was particular, specifically limited and limiting: my birthright was vast, connecting me to all that lives, and to everyone, forever. But one cannot claim the birthright without accepting the inheritance."[3] Each of us inherits a particular set of circumstances, from the time period and culture we live in to the specific woundedness of our family systems. We are called to do the healing work necessary to process those circumstances. We are also given the birthright, which is expansive and full of possibility. Mythologist Michael Meade describes this as the difference between fate and destiny.[4] Fate is what we are given at birth as the limitations of our lives. Destiny is where we aim our lives toward infinite possibility. We journey with both these realities.

When we begin to do ancestral work, we may find enormous clarity and wisdom by reconnecting to our lineages, but we will also encounter the unhealed and unresolved wounds that have been left to us as well. Toko-pa Turner says that this "convergence of ancestral momentum into a single body can be both confounding and liberating."[5] She goes on to write, "It's important to remember ourselves as the expression and extension of a long line of survivors. Our lives are but a continuation of all those who came before. In that way, their wounds are our own, in that it is up to us to make something of them. It is liberating to consider that when we heal an ancestral pattern, we are healing backwards through time, liberating all those souls who were left unresolved, unforgiven and misunderstood."[6]

We are responsible for doing the necessary work to help heal our ancestors because we are a part of them. We carry the wounds within us even if they remain unconscious.

Theologian Barbara Holmes, in her book *Joy Unspeakable*, says, "There is no response, other than radical love, that is up to the task of healing transgenerational wounds. The healing begins within. Questions that we lay on those inner altars and that receive no response in one generation are handed down to the next."[7] We must call upon the profound love that is available to us through the Divine Presence as well as our relationships that we have been cultivating with the angels, saints, and our already wise and loving ancestors.

Dr. Daniel Foor, when writing about healing ancestral wounds, notes two things I greatly value: the wisdom to call on ritual protection when working with the unwell spirits of the dead, and that the healing work is actually done by the wise and well ancestors themselves.[8] We just show up and empower it to happen through our loving care and attention.

During the last few years, I have integrated a practice of creating a sacred boundary around me when engaging with my ancestors and asking the Sacred Source; the Spirit; Christ; Mary as Protectress; the archangels, especially Michael the sacred warrior; and the saints to all help me create that boundary and allow only those ancestors who are truly well into my interior field. Much in the way we work to keep firm boundaries with humans who are unwell in this world, we can keep the energy of unwell ancestors from affecting our own.

WHY DO WE DO THIS WORK?

Family wounds are carried unconsciously from generation to generation and are in need of healing. The stories of our grandmothers and grandfathers are our stories. There is a great pool of wisdom available to us if we take the risk to dive in, because we can help to heal the wounds of the past and in the process heal ourselves by telling those stories again, giving voice to the voiceless, the unnamed, and the secrets, as well as to the celebrations, insights, and wisdom gathered over time.

We also honor the way the landscape, language, and culture have shaped the stories we've told, the words used to express the most aching sorrows and the most profound joys. We honor how ancestral lands with their trees, rivers, oceans, and undulations have been imprinted on our psychic lives and our souls.

Jung wrote extensively about the *collective unconscious*, which is this vast pool of ancestral memory within each of us; it is a kind of deposit of ancestral experience. He believed it comprises the psychic life of our ancestors right back to the earliest beginnings.[9] Nothing is lost; all of the stories, struggles, and wisdom are available to us. Each of us is an unconscious carrier of this ancestral experience, and part of our journey is to bring this to consciousness in our lives. He even believed it comprises our animal ancestry, which existed longer in time than our human existence. It is the place where archetypes emerge—those symbols and experiences that appear across time and cultures. The stories of our ancestors are woven into the fabric of our very being.

These teachings were expanded on by Murray Bowen, a psychiatrist in the twentieth century who developed concepts about how anxiety is dealt with in relationship systems. These concepts are known as Bowen family systems theory. The central idea is that patterns of relationship are transmitted from generation to generation, and once you become aware of the ways your family system has operated, you can change the system by not participating in the established responses to anxiety. This work has applications to larger systems of relationships as well and has been used often in congregations and in helping pastors to deal in healthy ways with community members, rather than falling into their own established relationship patterns.

Through the concept of *multigenerational transmission process*, Bowen believed that patterns are passed down genetically. An essential part of the work he advises is to establish relationship with as many living family members as possible to hear their stories and become familiar with what these patterns might be. One level of this work that has captivated me the most is the idea of our sacred stories being woven into a much larger tapestry of the generations that came before. We live in a very individualistic culture, in which not much honor is given to our ancestors and very little attention is paid to the stories that ripple through our very genetic code from generations that have gone before. I see our stories as embedded within the multiple layers of ancestral stories as well as within the larger cultural stories of which they are a part and then, even more broadly, the sacred story of Earth and the cosmos.

This multigenerational transmission process invites us to consider legacies of family patterns: "How we live and interact with those around us now is the result of an inherited prescription handed down through generations. In moving away from the cause-and-effect approach of Freud and others, Bowen moved closer towards a biblical anthropology and its understanding of the interconnectedness of humans. . . . A person can only be understood when considered in their position in a network of relationships, spanning the generations."[10] We are embedded in communities across both space and time.

Similar to this understanding of the impact of inherited patterns and ways of being in the world is the growing field of epigenetics, which studies how your behaviors and the environment you live in can cause changes that affect the ways your genes work. Dr. Rachel Yehuda has studied the children of Holocaust survivors and of pregnant women who survived the attacks on September 11, 2001. She learned that trauma can be transmitted biologically. The children of these survivors had a far greater likelihood of experiencing post-traumatic stress disorder as well as anxiety and depression. They were born with a greater biological vulnerability to stress. Trauma causes markers on genes, which get transmitted to children. The pain and suffering do not always diminish with time. Fragments of these traumatic life events live on in memory and body sensation, and they seek resolution from those living with them in the present who might not even realize they carry them. However, she points out that epigenetic changes are reversible, so any multigenerational impact can be altered. We are not doomed to repeatedly relive those patterns.

Dr. Yehuda goes on to observe that when people have something significant happen in their lives, they describe themselves as changed. What she thinks it means "is that the environmental influence has been so overwhelming that it has forced a major constitutional change, an enduring transformation. And epigenetics gives us the language and the science to be able to start unpacking that."[11] For all its negative effects, trauma can also positively create more strength and resilience in our genes that is passed down to future generations.

This understanding of trauma can help us have more compassion with our parents and grandparents for how they coped in their lives. It can also help us to be more compassionate with ourselves when we recognize how we have been affected by what happened in prior generations.

Carl Jung wrote in *Memories, Dreams, Reflections* about his sense of this in his own life:

> I became very aware of the fateful links between me and my ancestors. I feel very strongly that I am under the influence of things or questions which were left incomplete and unanswered by my parents and grandparents and more distant ancestors. It often seems as if there were an impersonal karma within a family, which is passed on from parents to children. It has always seemed to me that I had to answer questions which fate posed to my forefathers, and which had not yet been answered, or as if I had to complete, or perhaps continue, things which previous ages had left unfinished.[12]

We find this image of inheritance in the book of Exodus in the Hebrew Scriptures. Moses brings the stone tablets down from Mount Sinai, and God proclaims that while the Holy One forgives transgressions, "by no means clearing the guilty, but visiting the iniquity of the parents upon the children and the children's children, to the third and the fourth generation" (Ex 34:7b).

In the book of Jeremiah, it says that the days are coming when the people will build up and plant and it will no longer be said that "the parents have eaten sour grapes, and the children's teeth are set on edge" (Jer 31:29). At this time of the new covenant, people will start to take responsibility for their traumas and be sure they are no longer passed down to their children.

When our grandmothers were five months pregnant with our mothers, the cell of the egg from which you would develop was already there in your mother's ovaries. Before your mother was even born, you were sharing biological traces with your mother and grandmother. Similarly, the earliest cells of the sperm in your father from which you would be created were present when he was in his mother's womb. Science reveals to us that both the early sperm and the early egg can be imprinted with events that go on to affect following generations.[13] We are the recipients of our grandmother's nurturing (or lack thereof) through our mother. Any traumas she experienced and unresolved sorrow, loss, and pain will be transmitted to our mothers and to us. Our mothers would have been affected by their grandmothers and so on back through the lineage. We have the opportunity and responsibility to either continue a legacy of love or bring love back into the system.

Buddhist mindfulness teacher Thich Nhat Hanh described this healing process as the work of learning to love our inner child: "Our wounded child is not only us; he or she may represent several generations of ancestors. Our parents and ancestors may have suffered all their lives without knowing how to look after the wounded child in themselves, so they transmitted that child to us. So when we're embracing the wounded child inside us, we're embracing all the wounded children of past generations. This practice doesn't just benefit us; it liberates numberless generations of ancestors and descendants. This practice can break the cycle."[14]

These cycles, though, are easy for us all to fall in, as Bert Hellinger explored in his body of work called "Family Constellations." He believed that unconscious loyalties were at the heart of most suffering in families, as people repeat the patterns of their parents due to a hidden need to not betray them by living in a different way. He uses the term "entanglement" to describe the suffering that comes from carrying the burden of symptoms and pain of a previous family member as if it were your own.[15] For example, Dr. Joy Mannen, in her book *Family Constellations: A Practical Guide to Uncovering the Origins of Family Conflict*, gives the example of a grandfather who had affairs while his wife, the grandmother, put up with it out of fear of divorce and loss of social standing. She let her anger make her a victim of circumstance. Her granddaughter might be entangled with her grandmother's pain and suffering and not be able to sustain a relationship in her own life.[16]

Even if we have no conscious knowledge or memory of stories from our personal lineage, those memories still unconsciously live on within us in our psyche. Where they live would be the shadow parts of ourselves that we have inherited. Jung described it this way: "The psychogenesis of the spirits of the dead seems to me to be more or less as follows. When a person dies, the feelings and emotions that bound his relatives to him lose their application to reality and sink into the unconscious, where they activate a collective content that has a deleterious effect on consciousness."[17]

A great book to explore this work in epigenetics and how we can begin to heal ourselves is Mark Wolynn's *It Didn't Start with You*. The book focuses on "identifying inherited family patterns—the fears, feelings, and behavior we've unknowingly adopted that keep the cycle of suffering alive from generation to generation—and also how to end this cycle."[18]

Wolynn offers this image of how we are part of a great current of life that can get blocked if our relationship to our parents has been wounded in some way: "As children of our parents, we are connected to something vast that extends backward in time, literally to the beginning of humanity itself. Through our parents, we are plugged into the very current of life, though we are not the source of that current. The spark has merely been forwarded to us—transmitted biologically, along with our family history. It's also possible to experience how it lives inside us. This spark is our life force."[19]

Part of our ongoing inner work is to help heal this unconscious suffering by removing the constrictions to this flow in our lives. When we have some kind of block in our relationship with our parents, this life force will feel limited or as if we have to struggle for everything. He invites a visualization of an experience of welcome and openness between you and your biological parents. If this doesn't feel like a free flow, get in touch with how much the current is able to travel through you.

Some of the unconscious themes that block this life flow are overidentifying with a parent, rejecting a parent, experiencing a break in our earliest bond with our mother, or identifying with someone in our family system who is not a parent.[20] Wolynn says that any of these patterns can block our ability to flourish and can show up in many different aspects of our lives. Our parents are the portal to the creative force and the wounds we all carry in our ancestral legacy. I highly recommend his book to go deeper into healing the family wounds we carry through imagery and written exercises. It is potent work and beyond the scope of this book to explore all of his approaches.

Toko-pa Turner describes the impact of the healing work we do for ourselves: "It is liberating to consider that when we heal an ancestral pattern, we are healing backwards through time, liberating all those souls who were left unresolved, unforgiven and misunderstood."[21]

We do this work on behalf of our own healing, but we also do it on behalf of generations of ancestors who carried wounds they could not heal themselves in their lifetimes. We also do this on behalf of the wider collective, because our individual and ancestral healing has an impact on the community.

CALM OBSERVANCE

We are each affected in a profound way by the strands of our stories. My own ancestry can be traced back through four main lines: Austrian and Latvian on my father's side and England and Puritan New England on my mother's side. The more I explored, the more I could see how the trauma of war ripples through time, especially World War II for my father and World War I and the Civil War on my mother's side as family members were killed in these wars. Your ancestry will also have unique stories.

A core directive of family systems theory is to run not in the other direction of family trauma and pain but instead right back into the family system to understand it better. However, you must do so from a place of safety, anchoring, and calm observance. Understand the patterns of anxiety so you don't have to engage in them anymore. From this place, you no longer need to react from old wounds. This work demands courage to face the full legacy of your family stories, with all of their joy and sorrow. And when you reenter the family system from this perspective, the system itself begins to change.

My relationship with my father was fraught. Sadly, he was a man who struggled with many addictions, including alcohol and gambling. We had become estranged before he died. I am not like my father in many ways, but his story is still woven into my own. And of course he left me with many gifts as well. I carry the grief and pain of his having to flee the country of his upbringing for another land at a formative age during World War II, a story he would never utter. Knit into my being are the unfulfilled longings that propelled him forward, the wounds that haunted him. It is my responsibility to continue narrating these sacred ancestral stories with a tenderness and care for the traumas they hold.

We can't simply run away from the pain of our families; we can't escape the drama and dysfunction of human relationship. Our bones carry an ancestral narrative, and our sinews are studded with these tales. Our task is *not* to forgive and forget or to act as though the abuse perpetrated is not important. Our task *is* to walk calmly and courageously back into that system with open eyes and loving compassion.

Both my parents have died, and I have no siblings, so to go back to my family systems, I reach out to other family members, I walk again in ancestral landscapes and look with new eyes, and I enter back into my imagination and listen with new ears for what happened in their stories. I have conversations in my mind with ancestors. I gaze at photos of family members, looking for clues. I cherish the few photos I have where my parents, and especially my father, look joyfully at me—this new life for which he is responsible. I meditate with images of my father and me walking in the mountains of Austria. I read books about the cultural stories that have shaped my ancestors. I honor this web I am woven into.

After my father died, I went to visit his twin sister, my aunt Ieva, who lived in Brussels with her husband. It was always remarkable to me how different she was from my father, how much more resilient she seemed and how she was not chained to addiction to cope with life's challenges. She knew about his struggles and sympathized; as his twin, she felt enormous love for him. She shared with me stories of him as a child and whom she saw him to be at heart. She emphasized how much he loved me even though he couldn't always show it and how proud he always was of my accomplishments. Ieva told me about fleeing by train from Riga to Vienna when they were children and the Russians had occupied their homeland. How they had to leave their father behind, not knowing if he would be able to join them, and how they didn't realize they would never be returning home again. The compassion I felt for my father flowed so freely, and beautiful, healing tears came.

The call of this work is to walk back into the family system and embrace the reality of what *is*, asking why, and looking at it as an essential part of yourself rather than dismissing stories from the ancestors who have hurt you or whom you don't want to acknowledge. Ask yourself, What of this ancestral narrative have I disowned that calls to me to be reclaimed? What are the wounds I carry that need healing?

Love Has Come for You

In 2011, when I lived in Seattle, I began the process of applying for Austrian citizenship through my father and had to travel to the Austrian embassy in Los Angeles to submit my paperwork in person. My husband and I were seriously considering a sabbatical year in Vienna, which of course then turned into a move of our entire lives to Europe.

Citizenship would facilitate a number of things for our sabbatical year, but more than that, the act of obtaining citizenship was the culmination of my own inner journey over many months initiated by my experience at Christmas in 2010 when I arrived in Vienna alone and four days later found myself in the hospital with a pulmonary embolism. An embolism is a condition of the blood, and I was there to deepen my connection to my bloodline, so in a strange way, it thrust me even deeper into my journey.

My decision to finally apply for Austrian citizenship was another step on the road to healing and claiming that part of myself more fully. There was the practical reality of a new passport and rights conveyed to me, but there was also the spiritual reality of exploring where I owe allegiance within myself. A passport literally means a pass through a portal. Portals are liminal spaces charged with meaning and significance. You can never fully know how crossing that threshold will change you.

I had gathered the paperwork for months: birth, marriage, and death certificates for myself and my parents with the Apostille, a special certification process that required more letters and more waiting, including finding my father's alien registration card to prove he never naturalized as an American citizen. I flew down to submit it in person so they could take my fingerprints for the passport.

On the airplane returning home I was tired. Rather than tend to the pile of work I had brought with me, I decided to listen to some music and tend to my inner space in the wake of this journey I had just made. The song "Ten Thousand Angels" by Caedmon's Call started playing, and I heard these words: "How long you have traveled in darkness weeping . . . love has come for you."

Tears silently streamed down my cheeks, and I wiped them quietly away with my hand. There I was, thirty thousand feet in the air, suspended between heaven and earth, having just returned from a concrete act of saying yes to this part of myself, and my father and I were dancing in my imagination. Even more than that, when I heard the words to the song I knew they were about my father. *Love has come for him*. I knew they were about me. *Love has come for me*.

Rabbi Tirzah Firestone asks, "Is it possible to transform the effects of historical trauma? To come through life's heavy blows with more wisdom and a sense of inner freedom?" Then she follows with, "The answer is yes."[22] Healing is a process, and I continue to experience deeper and deeper freedom. I believe my ancestors who need healing also experience that freedom.

When Healing Comes

In May 2016, John and I traveled to Vienna, Austria, to lead a pilgrimage group, and while there, we spent some time at the beautiful Central Cemetery. This is where my father is buried alongside his parents. I visited his grave and encountered there a cuckoo bird circling from tree to tree, calling out again and again for perhaps an hour. I had never had an encounter like this before with my father's spirit, and I spent some time praying with this messenger. The cuckoo bird is unique in that it lays its eggs in the nest of another bird, allowing that bird to raise its young. It is a trickster bird. Even as I prayed with this messenger, I wondered what this meant.

On October 19, 2016, the thirteenth anniversary of my mother's death, I went to receive a massage from a very gifted woman in Galway where I live. I had a waking dream while lying on the table in the liminal space between waking and sleeping. I had been dealing with a difficult situation, and my father appeared to me saying that the eggs that had been given to me were not mine to mind and doing so would take away the nurturing from my own new birthings. I began to weep at this gift of clarity.

The waking dream continued. My father then asked me for an embrace, and I felt such an overflow of love toward him as I have never experienced. I could suddenly see him as both his innocent child self and the grown man he had become. His parents also appeared and encircled us both with their embrace. I saw this gorgeous light in the distance, the stunning gold light of October sun. I said to the three of them that they didn't need to stay here any longer; they could walk toward the light, and so they did.

The massage ended, and I lay there for several minutes on the table, savoring this encounter. After I got dressed and went out to see my massage therapist, she said that she felt my father's presence in the room and this beautiful golden light surrounding us both. I was stunned, because I had said nothing to her of the dream and there is no way she could have known what had transpired. It was a gift of confirmation.

He had died twenty years, seven months, and thirteen days prior. I had spent so many hours reaching toward him and my ancestors. I had moved to Vienna for a time to grow closer to his spirit. I had traveled and researched and opened my heart. It felt like such a gift of healing after years of inner work. Like the story of Jacob wrestling with the angel I shared earlier, I endured and eventually I was blessed.

I believe, along with Jung, that the stories of our ancestors run through our blood and the unhealed wounds and unfulfilled longings continue to propel us forward or keep us stuck in old patterns. The stories of our grandmothers and grandfathers are our stories, and we can help heal the wounds of the past and in the process heal ourselves by telling those stories again, giving voice to the voiceless, to the unnamed secrets, and to the celebrations, insights, and wisdom gathered over time.

Jung introduced us to the concept of the collective unconscious, that vast pool of ancestral memory within each of us. It is a kind of deposit of ancestral experience. He believed it comprises the psychic life of our ancestors right back to the earliest beginnings. Nothing is lost; all of the stories, struggles, and wisdom are available to us. Each of us is an unconscious carrier of this ancestral experience, and part of our journey is to bring this to consciousness in our lives.

ANCESTRAL LINEAGE HEALING

As I mentioned earlier, it is the wise and well ancestors who are the ones who heal our family lines. We simply invite in their presence. This does not mean we relinquish our responsibility for doing our own inner work and freeing ourselves from destructive patterns, but it does mean that we are not burdened with the responsibility of healing generations of wounds ourselves.

I included the chapter on working with the blessings of our ancestors before this one for precisely this reason. We begin by connecting to those wise and well ones, the bright and benevolent grandmothers and grandfathers who have crossed the veil and come into the fullness of love. Then we have the resources we need to call upon them to bring healing to our family lines.

Calling on our wise and well ancestors is another way to engage in this ancestral work as it brings the added dimension of seeking the support of those in our family line who are already resilient and can share their love and wisdom freely with us. After years of doing the hard work of healing on my own, with the support of my therapist, it was such a gift and grace to realize I had this wellspring of resources behind me, ready and willing to help me. It helped to heal one of my old wounds, which was an overbearing sense of over-responsibility and burden for keeping everything going. I was already in a process of softening these wounds and learning to yield myself more deeply to the Creator's embrace of me. I was undoing my patterns that had exhausted me for years. This was another layer of that healing work—to hand over even this need to heal, as if that were my work and not the work of Spirit anyway.

I think of this process of ancestral lineage healing as grounding myself in those who dwell across the veil and are intimately connected with Spirit already. These are the ones who came before me and remember that Love is the first and foundational reality. All else springs forth from this. This too is a process that takes time and ongoing communication.

PRACTICE
Humility and Conversion

Humility is one of the Benedictine commitments. It is a value that seems outdated in our world of self-empowerment and self-esteem boosting, negating much of the me-first values that our culture holds so dear. Of course, we want to be cautious about a humility that is promoted only to encourage passivity or low self-worth. These would be types of false humility.

Life-giving humility, in contrast, remembers the root of the word: *humus*, which means *earth*. Humility is at heart about being well-grounded and rooted. Humility is also about truth-telling and radical self-honesty. It is about celebrating the gifts we have been uniquely given in service of others as well as recognizing our limitations and woundedness. Humility is an act of love toward ourselves and to others.

Humility demands that we also celebrate our blessings as a part of truth-telling. It teaches us to recognize that our gifts are not of our own making but rather gifts we receive and hold in trust to give to our communities. Our gifts are not for ourselves alone. We are called to create not for our own satisfaction but to participate in the cocreation of a more just and beautiful world.

We can bring humility to this work of ancestral healing. We can honor our earthiness as human beings, doing the best we can in our lives and recognizing that our ancestors were also trying to survive and thrive in the ways they knew how.

Humility also calls us to the hard work of helping to heal those patterns, of which we likely weren't the originators, but it is now our path to do so. It is also honoring that we do this work with the support of God, the angels, saints, and wise and well ancestors.

Conversion is also a Benedictine commitment; it is the call to always be growing and changing. In contemplative practice, the interior movement is to grow in our capacity for love; we expand our hearts to be able to welcome more and more into our loving gaze. This begins with ourselves; we cultivate compassion for our own desires and longings and the choices we have made. We are then gradually able to see those who were invisible to us and give them the dignity of our attention. As we grow in this capacity for conversion, we begin to encounter God in more places and experiences. We open ourselves to being surprised by God in the moments when our hearts previously would have been closed.

When we commit to conversion, we commit to a continual process of growth, of stumbling over and over and getting up again, and of risking looking foolish because of something we are passionate about. We discover that the greatest transformations happen when we are willing to step into the unknown space between our egos and our deepest longings. Conversion is central to creativity because it calls us to begin again and again and try new things.

These twin practices of humility and conversion can help sustain us on this path of deep inner work, undoing the effects of traumas of the past. Some of the wounds we will never know the source of, only how they affect our lives. With humility, we can keep showing up in all our imperfections and continue on this healing journey. We can honor the ways our ancestors may have tried to heal themselves. Conversion calls us to stay with the work and to recognize that we never reach a place where we are done with it all. It is the work of a lifetime. We will continue to find new places where the current of that creative life force does not flow as freely as it should.

MEDITATION
Calling on the Support of the Wise and Well Ones for Healing

Find a comfortable seated position and deepen your breathing to help slow your awareness down. Imagine you are calling back all the tentacles of attention your mind has extended out to past and future—plans you are making, conversations you are rehearsing, and regrets you are experiencing. Draw your awareness back to yourself and this moment as much as possible. Bring your attention to your heart center, and rest in that inner sanctuary space for a few moments, connecting to the God of compassion. Bask for some time in that space of loving care from the One who created you. Allow yourself some time to simply be, rather than needing to do anything. We might think this healing work is ours to do, but ultimately, it is the Holy One, the angels, the saints, and the wise and well ancestors who all help support this healing journey.

In your imagination, invite back the wise and well ancestor you encountered in the meditation from the previous chapter. Spend some time together in one another's company. Tell this beloved ancestor of the healing you are seeking. Name the specific family member or situation you want to tend to; let them know what you are holding in your heart. Listen for the wisdom they respond with.

Ask them to surround this person and relationship with golden healing light. Let this unfold as it needs to in your imagination, allowing the ancestor to be the guide for the healing process. This may happen all at once, or it may be something you need to return to over time. Listen for what your ancestor says and needs. You can also invite in one of the saints, if there is one you feel a special connection with, and one of the angels or archangels—your guardian angel perhaps, or Michael, Gabriel, Raphael, or Uriel. See the three of them—ancestor, saint, and angel—calling on the power of the Spirit of healing to bring freedom and ease to this wounded one.

Once they have sent healing energy to this situation, rest a while together and ask if there is anything they would like you to do to help this healing work continue. Is there an action, ritual, prayer, or other offering you can do in the coming days? Listen for what that might be. Commit to this practice as part of your healing work. Return to this meditation as needed to bring more healing to persons in your lineage who need tending. At some point, you can even ask for healing for entire lines of the family tree.

Bring yourself gently back to the room you are in, and allow some time to reflect, journal, and decide how to continue the practice you have been called to do.

CREATIVE EXPLORATION
Write a Blessing for Your Ancestors

You are invited to write a blessing for the angels, saints, and ancestors. This is a prayer you can read as part of your meditation time that is dedicated to cultivating a relationship with those in the invisible world.

Many of the people who came before us struggled mightily with life circumstances, loss, addiction, and other sorrow or suffering. As you delve deeper into the stories of those who came before you, you may begin to recognize the way you continue to carry those unresolved layers of grief in your marrow.

Take some time to bless each of your ancestors by name, wishing healing for them and the graces they would have needed, knowing what life had dealt to them. You might want to express these spontaneously out loud or write them down as they come to you.

A Blessing for Healing

You know there are still ruptures
across the generations,
the wounds of loss, betrayal, violence.
Ask the Beloved
and the ancient ones to bring healing.

Whisper with them to the wounded ones:
May you find yourselves
dancing among trees and swimming
in a vast sea of love.
May you be healed
from the painful wounds of your earthly life.
May you encounter
the deep peace of your dreams
and may the joy hidden in your
blood and bones be released
to ripple across time.
Blessed be your memory,
and in my act of remembering,
may I help to untangle the knotted threads,
allowing them to dissolve,
release the secrets and shame,
let them be transmuted through grace.
May you dance in your birthright,
may the joy remain, fill the hollow spaces within,
may you be set free from the binding of your struggles,
may you receive the gifts of your wisdom,
and may you be woven together
into a vast community of love.

9

GRIEVING OUR LOSSES

Fear not the pain. Let its weight fall back
into the earth,
For heavy are the mountains, heavy the seas.

—Rainer Maria Rilke, from *Sonnets to Orpheus*

In the spring of 2022, just five days before I was due to travel from Ireland to Austria to have major surgery, my aunt Nancy became very ill and was terminating treatment. Her husband, my uncle Larz, called me to prepare me for the reality that she would be dying in a matter of days.

I was always very close with my aunt, my mother's younger sister. She never had children of her own and had always taken it upon herself to be one of my great supports and cheerleaders in life. She was always supportive and encouraging, and after my mother died, we continued to stay close through emails, phone calls, and visits whenever I was back in the States.

The summer before, she had been diagnosed with stage IV breast cancer that had spread to her spine; however, her oncologist put her on medication to slow the progress and said that in older age cancer grows much more slowly anyway. Because the pandemic was still raging and my aunt was now a vulnerable person, I didn't feel comfortable traveling from Ireland back to Maine to see her. I was also dealing with some complicated health issues that made the decision to travel unwise.

I made sure to keep up communication, and she always sounded in good spirits. When March 2022 came, I began to consider a trip to visit her in the summer in the hopes that the pandemic would be in a place where I could do so in relative safety.

But then I received a call from my uncle, first letting me know she was in the hospital and had to have surgery to remove fluid from her heart. I called her there, and she could barely speak between gasping breaths. She kept saying, "It's so good to hear your voice." I told her I loved her and continued to hold her in prayer.

The next day the hospital performed surgery to drain the fluid, but it didn't go well. She developed an infection and became so ill by Friday that she chose to withdraw all further medical treatment. Larz called me in the middle of the night to let me know. He was of course heartbroken to be losing his beloved. I was heartbroken I couldn't visit her one more time, especially that I couldn't be on the threshold with her. With my trip to Austria to address my own health issues in a few days, I knew it wouldn't be possible to cancel everything to be by her side. Even if I could, I knew that she would likely die while I was still in transit anyway. Because Larz had his own health issues, he would not be able to stay by her side in the hospital.

One of the most profound experiences of my life was sitting vigil with my mother as she lay dying. My heart hurt at imagining Nancy alone there in her hospital bed, ready to let go. I realized in these moments that I had to sit vigil with Nancy from a distance. I could still help midwife her across the veil from where I was even though an ocean separated us.

That weekend I prayed with and for her throughout the hours that passed. I called first on her sister's presence. I knew my mother would be standing at the veil ready to welcome Nancy with open arms. I had already been praying with St. Francis's Sister Death for some weeks as I prepared for my own surgery. Sister Death is a potent reminder of our mortality and the gift that comes from intimate connection to her. And only a few days before this experience I had been introduced to a new face of Mary, Our Lady of a Good Death, a Black Madonna who sits in the gothic cathedral of Clermont-Ferrand in France.[1] My mother, Sister Death, Mary, and Michael the archangel, who is said to help shepherd souls through that bright doorway, all joined me in this transition time. I prayed and sang and wept. I felt the Divine Presence as a great golden light, something I have experienced with previous loved ones who have died. I wailed at my loss, knowing I would not see her again on this plane of physical existence.

As those of you who have sat with loved ones as they transitioned to death know, the veil between worlds at those moments is very thin and time seems to stand still. Barbara Holmes describes this time outside of time well: "The abiding time that precedes death can be deeply contemplative moments in which space-time has no meaning. Boundaries can be crossed at will, granting us the ability to abide with one another in the spiritual landscape that grace allows."[2] Even though I was not in her physical presence, boundaries of space did not matter in those moments.

That Sunday morning, I awoke from a dream. In it, my aunt appeared to me as a much younger woman surrounded by a beautiful light. She was reaching her hand toward me telling me everything was okay and inviting me to dance. A couple of hours later, I received the call from Larz that she had indeed passed.

I flew the next day to Vienna, Austria, for my hysterectomy. I had two weeks of preparatory appointments, and perhaps because of the surrealness of it all, I hadn't yet really opened my heart to the grief.

The day before my surgery, I checked into the hospital. That night I didn't sleep well, so I spent most of the hours praying for my own procedure and the best outcome. I could feel my mother and my aunt there, standing on either side of me and midwifing me into new ease. And then the tears came in a rush, streaming down my face each night following the surgery after the nurses would turn out the lights. I would lie in my hospital bed silently choking on tears, listening to music on my phone that helped to channel my grief.

Thankfully my surgery went very well. I had a hysterectomy to remove a very large fibroid that had caused pain and discomfort for years. Releasing the fibroid and my uterus felt like a powerful connection to a release of wounding in my motherline, something ancient I couldn't name. I was weeping in both sadness over my losses and equally a sense of joy at new connection. I felt connected to generations of mothers and grandmothers whose voices were subdued and suppressed yet who sang through the music I was listening to of the promise of rising again. They would rise in me and through me and around me, and I sensed I had nothing at all to fear. I midwifed my aunt at death, and now she was midwifing me to restored health and fuller life.

GRIEF AND LOSS

Being in Vienna, mourning my aunt, reminded me of another time I was in Austria mourning the death of my mother. One of the most amazing places I have ever visited was the bone chapel in Hallstatt, Austria. Hallstatt is a beautiful little village tucked between mountain and lake. Bones from the cemetery used to be removed to make room for the newly dead. The skulls were bleached in the sun and then lovingly hand-painted by family members with names, dates, and decorations. Standing in the room with six hundred skulls was a transcendent experience. I was brushing against my own mortality, confronted with my own vulnerable body made up of bone and fragile tissue, and at the same time witnessing the beauty of what remains. I imagined what it would be like to hold the skull of a loved one in my hands, to feel the hardness of bone, to be confronted with the reality of death, and then to illuminate that reality with art and beauty.

I shared about my mother's death in an earlier chapter. After she died, I felt bereft for a long time. I missed the ordinary exchanges: sitting and drinking coffee with her in the mornings as we sometimes did and sharing the deep joys and struggles of our lives, the color of her lipstick, the scent of her perfume, and even those times when I had to help her get dressed because her body had deteriorated.

There were two images from scripture that came to me during that time of mourning. The first was a line from the psalms: "You have collected all my tears in your bottle" (Ps 56:8, NLT). I imagined that God would need a vessel the size of the ocean to gather all the tears I had shed. The second was from the Gospel of Matthew (2:18), which refers back to the Hebrew Scriptures—Rachel was weeping for her children, and *she would not be consoled* because her children were no more. There is tremendous power in allowing our grief to be unleashed and not letting our cries be silenced.

During that first year of grieving my mother, I attended a concert for the Feast of All Soul's, and one piece of music in particular moved me deeply: "An Caoineadh," which is Irish for "The Keen." As the program explained, keening is a specific type of wailing done over the body of the dead and was traditionally performed by women while rocking back and forth, calling the name of the dead relative or friend. It is a custom that dates back to pre-Christian funerals.

So often we are taught to subdue our grief, to hold back, and to move on. Yet what my intuition has taught me during these times of deep sorrow is to make room for it, to create a wide, welcoming space for the enormity of anguish, for the ocean of tears. In this way, we actually give honor to the person we lost; through our grieving we say that this person mattered deeply to us.

With the death of both my parents as well as John's parents, the deaths of other relatives and loved ones, and the loss of two beloved canine companions whom I held in my arms as they died, I am familiar with the landscape of loss. I know life's fragility in an intimate way. I know the terrible ache of grief when I have wondered how I can even manage to keep my lungs filled with air.

None of us is spared this experience. We may have to face it in a variety of ways—the loss of a job, a home, a dream, a beloved one, or many loved ones. Each can tear our hearts wide open if we let it.

Yet life is filled with paradox. In a world filled with losses and ending, there is also unspeakable beauty. For the many hours I have spent with my heart rended, I have spent as many hours in awe of a landscape, of a small kindness, and of love. To the degree I welcome in grief is also the degree to which I am capable of welcoming in joy. Life is unbelievably fragile and fleeting, *and* it is made of a substance that is solid like steel or stone, enduring in ways we had not imagined.

Honoring the ancestors means also honoring the grief and loss that comes when loved ones leave this life and pass into one with a different form. We lose their physical presence, a loss that can feel as if an echoing cavern has opened up inside of us. We may also grieve, as I did with my father for so many years, of not having had a life-giving relationship with a loved one because of their addictions and struggles. However, on the other side of grief, there can still be joy.

PRACTICE
Lament

Each one of us carries grief, sorrow that has perhaps gone unexpressed or been stifled or numbed. Each of us has been touched by pain and suffering at some time. Yet we live in a culture that tells us to move on, to get over it, to shop or drink our way through sorrow, or to fill our moments with the chatter of TV, radio, and smartphones so that we never have to face the silent desert of our hearts. It is the same kind of attitude that forces us to answer "fine" when others ask how we are, even when we really aren't. Even our churches often try to move us too quickly to a place of hope without fully experiencing the sorrow that pierces us.

In his book *Art + Faith*, artist and theologian Makoto Fujimura writes, "If we desire to be there with those whose incalculable losses outweigh any sentiments of hope, with those who are too ill to have a future, with those facing the darkness of depression, we need to know how that feels before we can endeavor to be present in suffering. We need to learn to lament and weep deeply for the reality all around us."[3] This is where the profound wisdom in our tradition of lament enters. The Hebrew Scriptures are filled with this prayer of crying out to God. Lament gives form and voice to our grief, a space to wail and name what is not right in the world in the context of prayer. Jesus laments on the Cross and cries out, "My God, my God, why have you forsaken me?" (Mt 27:46).

The theologian Walter Brueggemann writes about the need for lament in his book *The Prophetic Imagination*. He says that people can only dare to envision a new reality when they've been able to grieve, to scream out, and to let loose the cry that has been stuck in their throats for so long. That cry, the expression of that grief, says Brueggemann, "is the most visceral announcement that things are not right."[4] Only after we have released this lament can we begin "to nurture, nourish, and evoke a new consciousness,"[5] a new vision. We so desperately need a new way of seeing the world.

The prayer of lament is first and foremost truth-telling; it begins by challenging the way things are. Lament names that something is not right in the world. This pain, this suffering, should not be. It helps us to name the lies we have been living and participating in.

Lament opens us up to a new vision of how God is present to our suffering. We call on the God who weeps with us, whose groans are our own, and we express our hope in God's tender care.

Lament is a form of resistance: We allow ourselves to be present to God in our brokenness and resist the cultural imperative to be strong and hold it all together. We resist cultural practices of denying death through our worship of eternal youth. We stop pretending everything is okay and put an end to worshipping the status quo.

Lament puts us in solidarity with those who are suffering and schools us in compassion. Only when we have become familiar with the landscape of our own pain can we then enter into the suffering of another. Lament moves us beyond our own narrow perspectives.

In the prayer of lament, we help give voice to the oppressed, to hidden suffering, and the suffering in silence that happens because pain takes our language away. Gathered together, we say that the pain is being heard, that it is valid. Our community votes with its tears that there is suffering worth weeping over.

Finally, lament is the release of power, God's power—the power that is the soul-transforming call of repentance. The paradox of our faith is that we must first surrender fully to these ashes, into the desert places of brokenness, before Easter and its promise of resurrection can fully enter and fill us. Lament invites in God's reconciling and healing power.

MEDITATION
Making Room for Your Own Grief

After my mother died, I received a valuable suggestion from my spiritual director to make time each day for a specific period, about half an hour, to express my grief in whatever way it needed to come through. I would pause in the evenings as part of my night prayer and bring my mother's presence close to my heart. I'd call to mind Psalm 56:8, which says the One who grieves with us puts all of our tears in a vial. Sometimes I would play a piece of music that helped to create space for whatever feelings were moving inside me. Sometimes I would journal for a while about what I missed about my mother. Sometimes I just sat in silence and let myself feel the emptiness of missing her.

This was a helpful practice because, first, it gave me time and space to enter into my grieving process and give it room for expression. Second, it helped me to be able to function at work as I knew I had a place to bring my grief later in the day. Sometimes the grief did erupt in messy places; mourning is like that. It won't be controlled but can sometimes be lovingly contained. It helped me to show up day by day and tend to what was moving in my heart and soul.

I invite you to make a regular time in your own life for something you are grieving for right now. It may be the physical death of a loved one or it might be some other kind of loss, such as illness of yourself or another or loss of a job or dream. All of these are worthy of a ritual of time and space to dedicate to the grief process.

Begin by deepening your breath and grounding yourself by feeling your feet on the floor. Imagine sending roots deep into the earth beneath you. Invite in that sense of strength and stability that comes from being deeply rooted. Remember that if at any time you feel overwhelmed, you can step out of the meditation or return to this image of physical connection to the floor and, below that, the ground.

Start by naming the grief you want to honor. Then offer a prayer to open this time. It might be a breath prayer such as this:

Inhale: I surrender
Exhale: to sorrow.

With each inhale, repeat the words *I surrender* to yourself silently. With each exhale, repeat the words *to sorrow*. Let your exhale be full, perhaps even a heavy sigh. This kind of physical expression can open the gate for our tears to flow. Remember the God who pours our tears into a holy vessel.

Reflect on what your losses are: What about the presence of a loved one do you miss the most and grieve over its absence? The loss of a physical ability? The loss of a dream or plan?

As you feel emotion come up, try putting on a piece of music and letting your body move with it. Some suggestions are Samuel Barber's *Adagio for Strings* or Vivaldi's *Nisi Dominus* or some other favorite music that helps you get in touch with the more tender emotions. Invite your body into a prayer; see how your body wants to move. What would feel satisfying? Are there any sounds you want to make? Sometimes verbal expression of grief can be helpful and cathartic.

As the music subsides, let your breathing deepen again and return to being seated, giving yourself time to return to a quiet space within. You may want to spend some more time journaling following this experience. You might want to write a letter to the person you are missing and let them know all the specific things you miss about them.

CREATIVE EXPLORATION
Write an Elegy

An elegy is a reflection on death, either your own or the death of another. It is generally a lament for something lost. You could write an elegy for a loved one who has passed away, remembering their gifts. You could write an elegy for one of your own abilities you have lost, perhaps due to aging. You can also write an elegy for an aspect of nature that is dying or going extinct. This does not have to be a morbid exercise; instead, it can be one in which you celebrate life. Let this elegy offer joyful praise for the gift of presence in this world.

If you are writing it about yourself, in poetic form, celebrate what you have done for the world. In what ways will you be remembered? What did you build, create, or teach? How has your life affected others? How will those around you be changed by your presence?

If it is about another person, celebrate their gifts, what they brought to your life and the lives of others.

Blessing for Grief

This blessing sits with you in the ache
and dark cave of loss.
Let your voice ring out into the hollow space
of stone and bone,
a wail, a cry, a lament.
Call on wise ones to surround you,
Michael the Archangel,
Mary, Our Lady of Sorrow,
Sister Death,
and any other ancient ones
whose presence would be steadying.
You do not have to be consoled,
you do not have to hold back the river of tears,
you do not have to hold it all together.
Rest your spine back against the soft rock
and feel yourself held by Earth,
by the saints and ancestors
who knew their own landscape of loss.
Give yourself over to this holy time of grief,
a witness to the expanse of your love,

and when the heaviness is too much to bear,
ask the mountains and the oceans
to carry the weight in their enormous arms.
Notice all the places you still hold back
and soften, surrender, release.
Hear Jesus's cry of abandonment from the Cross
and know this mourning as part of your humanity.
Let this blessing carry you as well,
to the far distant shores of your longing.

10

ANCESTRAL PILGRIMAGE

Pilgrims are persons in motion—passing through territories not their own—seeking something we might call completion or perhaps the word clarity will do as well, a goal to which only the spirit's compass points the way.

—Richard R. Niebuhr

One of my primary spiritual practices over the last twenty years has been ancestral pilgrimage. As we explored in one of the chapters on the saints, pilgrimage is a journey of meaning to a sacred site. For an ancestral pilgrimage, the place has significance for the pilgrim's ancestors. I trace my genetic lineage back primarily through New England, England, Austria, the Czech Republic, Slovenia, and Latvia, and I have traveled to each of these places, sometimes multiple times, as part of my personal journey.

These journeys have changed me; they brought much healing to my life and called forth even more from me. After several of these ancestral pilgrimages, John and I moved to Vienna, the city where my father grew up and I spent time as a child, as a deeper commitment to continuing this ancestral journey. We were there for six months so that I could reconnect to something I wanted to reclaim for myself. I wanted to remember I was a daughter of that land.

A pilgrimage is a special kind of journey, one taken to a holy place with the hope of an encounter with the sacred and the intention of being changed by what happens there and along the way. We don't go on pilgrimages to return the same person.

I believe we are profoundly connected to the land, language, and culture of our ancestors in ways we don't fully realize. Their experiences, sorrows, and joys are knit into our bones, woven into the fabric of our very bodies. The impulse to discover one's story often leads us to reach far back into history. We perhaps can't fully understand the impact of these connections until we stand on the land, speak the language, and taste the food of those who came before us.

Each time I prepare for these journeys with excitement and anticipation, as well as fear and trembling, knowing I will have to confront the shadow sides of my family system. But it is in facing the dark depths that I no longer have to live in fear of them.

"If your journey is indeed a pilgrimage, a soulful journey, it will be rigorous. Ancient wisdom suggests if you aren't trembling as you approach the sacred, it isn't the real thing. The sacred, in its various guises as holy ground, art, or knowledge, evokes emotion and commotion," writes Phil Cousineau, in his book *The Art of Pilgrimage*.[1] Pilgrimage demands something of us and can shake our foundations as we connect to something meaningful and profound.

Pilgrimages are threshold times. Anthropologist Victor Turner writes about these thresholds as liminal spaces where our established patterns begin to come undone and we are thrust into a time of unknowing.[2]

If you have ever journeyed to an ancestral homeland, you have perhaps experienced this feeling of being in time outside of time and connecting to those who share your blood and bone, who walked those paths and were shaped by those landscapes. I know the first time I went to visit Latvia, where my father was born, the way the forest ran along the Baltic Sea stirred something deep in my heart I don't have words for. It was just a sense of knowing and aliveness in that place. I stood there at the edge of the Baltic Sea, on the beach at Jurmala in Latvia, and I felt a deep kinship to this place where I had never been before. Perhaps it was standing at this borderland place where forest meets the sea, the same kind of landscape I had fallen in love with in the United States' Pacific Northwest. Thousands of miles away, I had met this place of wildness and fallen in love. As I stood in this ancestral land, I felt a connection, a kind of deep knowing.

Maybe the felt connection was because of the photos I have of my father playing on these same sands, the carefree days of his childhood long before the burdens of adulthood settled into his bones and the deep grooves formed on his forehead. Maybe there was another reason for that feeling of connection. Whatever the source, walking this ancestral landscape brought me a sense of understanding and peace. My father had fled this country as a boy when the Russians invaded. He became a refugee, never to return home again in his entire life. I was making this journey in part on his behalf, to restore something that had been broken.

For so many of us, a disconnection from the land of our ancestors may be a significant contributor to the sense of exile we often feel. In her book *Belonging*, Toko-pa Turner invites us to consider how our bodies are made up of the same water, earth, and minerals as the earth we inhabit.

> It isn't difficult then, to make the leap into how the specificity of a geography, its quality of soil and water, climate and altitude, would change the evolutionary makeup of a people quite dramatically. For instance, how the wind in the mountains might broaden the shape of one's face, or how being closer to the sun might darken the skin, how constant cold might shape a nose to be long and narrow, to conserve heat. Just as land is shaped by the conditions of its place, we too are similarly landscaped.
> .... There is no separation from the place where we live, except for the one made by our own forgetting.[3]

To be able to stand in the land of your ancestors, breathe in the air, feel the quality of light, and stand on the stone and bedrock of the place is to return to an elemental awareness of what shaped our foremothers and forefathers. It is to vividly sense that elemental awareness that has been passed down to us in a kind of geological memory imprinted upon our souls, much in the same way as trauma and wounding can be.

That geological memory is part of how we feel connected. As Sandra Easter states, "One's sense of belonging is intimately connected with one's relationship with the ancestors and the land, and, with a reconnection with the 'archaic' part of the collective unconscious."[4] This "archaic" part is what Jung called the primeval self, the part of ourselves connected to ancient beings and ancestors, who were indigenous to the land they lived on. We experience a profound longing for wisdom stories passed down through generations. We desire to be immersed in that landscape where our ancestors felt a sense of belonging.

Ancestral Language

My father used to say that you lived as many lives as languages you spoke. He spoke Latvian, German, and English as well as actively studied other languages at various times of his life. He worked at the United Nations and valued travel and language as portals to new worlds.

One of my great regrets is that as a child I resisted speaking German at home. I had a difficult relationship with my father, so I think that was one way I rebelled against him. While I can get by well with my German-language skills in day-to-day life when in Austria, I do long to be fluent in a way that I will probably not be able to achieve in this life, still learning the language as an adult and not living in a German-speaking country. But I believe the effort I put in to continue my studies of German support this work of connecting to an ancient part of myself. Sometimes I read a word or phrase in German and can understand a whole different way of seeing the world.

As a child we traveled quite a bit, returning to Austria every year or so to visit family, but my German remained rusty from lack of regular practice. I regret those stubborn childhood ways. My father died soon after I finished college, and it was nearly twenty years before I had the opportunity to return to Vienna, during a five-week ancestral pilgrimage in 2009 with my husband.

Some of my most delightful moments have happened while in Vienna and making the effort to speak German with waiters or shop clerks and having a conversation. Making a connection with another across the boundary of language is one of the great joys we can find in expanding our horizons.

Speaking German again over our month of travel, even with all of my stumbling, touched something in me I still can't quite fully express. It opened up a longing in me, a riverbed of memories shaped by the words of another language. I could suddenly feel myself connected to generations of ancestors for whom German was the language of their longing. I began to discover that the shape and trajectory of those longings, longings that threaded through the cosmos, dwelled inside of me and called me forward. As I spoke in German with others, I was overcome by joy in discovering that my ability exceeded my self-perceived limits. I was also moved by grief as we neared the end of our trip and for my years of neglecting this language that beats in my blood.

I have continued to study German because something comes alive in me when I understand more of what is being said or written in a book I am reading. We might not become fluent in a language, but we can gain fluency of the heart by opening ourselves to these ways of connection.

Ich liebe dich in German. *Es mīlu Tevi* in Latvian. *Ljubim te* in Slovenian. *Miluji tě* in Czech. These are the words for "I love you" in some of the languages my ancestors spoke. I will never become fluent in Latvian, Slovenian, or Czech, but learning the words and meditating with them opens my heart to the love of thousands before me. It helps me feel how generations of ancestors whispered these words to one another, husband and wife, parents and grandparents to children, and other intimate, loving connections.

Through language I am slowly rediscovering within myself whole worlds I had forgotten were there. I feel as though I have reopened a locked room, one filled with dust but also radiant with sunlight that illuminates old, forgotten photos and letters. As my mouth forms these words, I become aware that these were the very sounds that emerged from the mouths of my ancestors to gently comfort one another, to whisper secrets, to cry out at night after a great heartrending loss, and to utter their most essential truths. The nuances of language express the soul of a people.

We'll discuss going on an ancestral pilgrimage more later in this chapter, as well as different ways to go on one. If you do go on ancestral pilgrimage, learn some phrases in the language of your people. Notice what it kindles in you to speak these words aloud. Even if you don't have a chance to travel to where your ancestors are from, learn some of those phrases your ancestors might have spoken. Hold them in your heart and say them aloud, feeling yourself to be a continuation of their loves, dreams, and longings.

ANCESTRAL NOURISHMENT

If you have ever traveled outside of your home country, you know the joys of eating new foods and discovering new flavors. Food is so much at the heart of cultural identity and family connections. Sitting down to a meal together and eating food made with love is a great pleasure and delight.

Food is one way that customs of a place are passed down from one generation to the next. It is a way of preserving a cultural identity. Even though my mother was American, having grown up near Boston, when she married my father she learned to speak German and cooked some Austrian dishes at home. *Kaiserschmarrn, Palatschinken, Knödel, Linzertorte*, and *Sachertorte* are some of the foods she would cook regularly that still kindle something in me when I eat them. My father's mother would have taught her a variety of Austrian delicacies, and I am grateful to my mother for continuing this lineage of food even though it wasn't her upbringing. It brings a profound sense of comfort and connection. I love going back to Vienna and having a really good Wiener schnitzel with *Preiselbeeren* and *Erdäpfelsalat*.

One of the dishes my mother cooked regularly to companion a main meal is *Rotkraut*, or braised red cabbage. It is something I still love to make. It takes some time to chop, combine, and cook but is worth the effort. The smell and taste transport me to being a little girl again in our New York City apartment, bringing Austria into our kitchen and dining room.

If you go on ancestral pilgrimage, let the local foods shape your experience. If you cannot travel, depending on where your ancestors are from, you may be able to eat in a local restaurant that serves food from that culture already. Or perhaps you have a family recipe for a favorite dish that you already like to prepare, like my *Rotkraut*. Let eating be a prayer of reconnection and communion with those who came before you.

PRACTICE
Ancestral Pilgrimage

Consider making a pilgrimage to walk in the footsteps of your own ancestors if possible, those everyday saints who struggled with life's heartaches and suffering. Spend time in the places that shaped their imaginations and their dreams; learn to speak some of the language with which they whispered their most private secrets to one another, the words they used to express their aching sorrow and profound joy. It doesn't matter if you know nothing of the details. Walking, being, listening, and noticing the impact of trees, rivers, mountains, and sky on your own spirit is enough.

Potawatomi writer and theologian Kaitlin Curtice reminds us of our own belonging to a land: "You may not be Native in the way that I am Native, but you belong to a people as you long for a space to know what it means to hold the realities of love, mystery, and hope. I pray that you find your own soul-origins, those origins that help you trace your steps back to those early moments of your being when you were formed and spoken to in the depths of your soul."[5] This image of finding our soul origins is so beautiful and profound. Ancestral pilgrimage is a journey to retrieve those soul origins and come to a deeper understanding of what has shaped us.

A pilgrimage doesn't have to be a long journey overseas. It might be to a nearby cemetery or a phone call with a living relative to ask about stories you have never heard before. It might mean simply looking up images online of the places you are from. It might mean searching for the word for *love* in the language your ancestors spoke and bringing that into your daily time of prayer.

If you are able to travel, rather than moving from city to city or place to place, linger in one place for several days. You are traveling not for the sake of checking destinations off of a list but to have a genuine encounter with a landscape and culture that might change you. Keep a journal of what you encounter and experience along the way. Notice synchronicities and write down your dreams. Often when we are seeking connection with our ancestors, the veil between worlds becomes thinner.

If you have a photo of your ancestor from this place, bring it with you. Read about the cultural history of the place: What were the events that shape its memory and beliefs? Learn a few words of the language. Sit in a café off the main tourist route and listen to people engaged in conversation around you. Imagine they are your ancestors. What do you hear?

MEDITATION
The Language and Taste of Love

To prepare for this meditation, I invite you to look up the words for *I love you* in the language of one of your ancestral lines. Sometimes you can find video or audio that helps with the pronunciation, but do the best you can. The desire and effort go a long way to honoring your ancestors. You might write the words on a card and carry it with you or place it on your altar so you can include those words in your prayer time. See if you can find a translation of a favorite prayer into the language; for example, if you are rooted in the Christian tradition with a love of Mary, perhaps you can find the words for the Hail Mary prayer in the language of your ancestors.

If you didn't grow up with an ancestral food tradition, consider looking online for recipes or purchasing a cookbook for the particular country or culture where you are from. Choose a recipe that calls to you somehow, whether because of the particular ingredients or a memory or longing it stirs within you. Trust your intuition. Make it something simple to begin; you can always work up to more complexity in time. Choose just one dish to learn how to prepare for this meditation. If you did grow up with an ancestral food tradition, choose a dish you always loved or one you cook often now, something that brings comfort and a sense of connection.

Before you begin cooking, offer this time of preparation and eating in honor of the ancestors from that particular land. Keep them in your mind and heart as you work through the recipe. Imagine the hands of great-grandmothers and great-grandfathers chopping and stirring and mixing and cooking.

As you sit down to eat, offer a brief meditation of gratitude for your ancestors; imagine them sitting down with you to enjoy this feast. Pray the words for *I love you* in your ancestral language, directing your words to your kin of blood and bone. Let the meal be a time of connection and celebration. Let it fill you with love.

If you enjoy the meal, you might practice it again and again until it becomes natural for you to bring the ingredients together.

CREATIVE EXPLORATION
Poetry Writing

We are going to use another poem as the jumping-off point for our own poetry writing. You might want to begin by searching online for "Kim Moore My People" and her poem from her collection *The Art of Falling* will show up in your results. That poem was the inspiration for my own below, and I invite you to use it as a starting point for your own poetic contemplation.

Read through my poem twice slowly:

> I come from people who dragged nets of fish
> from the Atlantic, could smell it on their hands
> and clothes long into the night.
>
> I come from people who stood at the shore
> of the Baltic Sea, watching Solstice bonfires
> in the waters, rippling outward.

I come from men wearing soldier's uniforms,
torn, blood-stained, medals rusting in the dresser.
I come from rabbis and ministers,
grocers and lawyers, businessmen
opening another new store.

I come from women who loved to teach and dance,
but once married were forbidden such
suspicious joys anymore, who danced in secret
before children awakened, hiding
calloused feet in slippers,
who told stories of the one room schoolhouse
and kept a piece of chalk in the drawer to smell.[6]

After you've read through the poem, give yourself ten minutes to freewrite about all the kinds of people you come from: the places they lived, the landscapes they inhabited, the kinds of jobs they held, and the people they loved. If you don't know any of these details, tune into your imagination and make it up as you go along. If you have ever done a DNA test, you might at the very least know the names of some of the countries you come from. From there, you can imagine the kinds of lives they lived and see what emerges.

Blessing for Ancestral Lands

Even if you never make the physical journey
to the lands of your ancestors,
those lands journey in you:
the rivers flow through your blood,
the mineral and stone in your bones,
the echo of the breezes in each breath,
the storms and sunshine radiating in your heart,
the rise and fall of tides with each pump,
a deep knowing of your original indigenous self.
Close your eyes and feel yourself arriving home
to remember your inheritance

as a child of the land.
And if your travels have brought you
on ancestral pilgrimage,
you know the courage and endurance demanded,
a dance between belonging and being adrift,
you know these weren't a mere passing through,
but an offering, a reaching into the past,
a carrying of treasure into the future.
Let this blessing open a door
into memory, pause and listen
to the language, the rumblings of earth,
the lulling of lakes, the way stone feels beneath your feet.
Find nourishment in the fruits of the table,
the grains kneaded into bread.
Give gratitude for this bit of ground
from which your ancestors emerged.
Know its contours as the shape of your dreams
and your most sacred imagination.

11

COSMOLOGY, MYTH, AND SONG

Living on the land one was born from and into—
where the bones of one's ancestors rest, where the
stories of one's ancestors and their wisdom sit in the
landscape—grounds, nourishes, and sustains a deep
sense of belonging, one in which body is connected
to earth and spirit through and within time and
space. A cosmology with creation stories and wisdom
stories, ceremonies and rituals, that come from the
land and have been passed down through countless
generations, provides a context which connects each
individual life through time and space and in time and
place to herself, her family, her clan, her nation, and to
that which is eternal.

—Dr. Sandra Easter, *Jung and the Ancestors*

Cosmology is essentially a worldview a culture holds about the origins
of life and its purposes. Myths help to illuminate the cosmology by
bringing story and image to life. One way we can connect to our

ancestors is to explore the cosmologies and cultures of the lands they came from.

Exploring the culture and stories of our ancestors helps us to encounter ways our ancestors might have experienced and understood life. We can enter into conversation with them and ask what they valued.

There are many ways to start to research what these stories might be. One helpful resource to start with is the Encyclopedia Mythica online (https://pantheon.org).[1] Folklore is essentially the body of a culture's myths, stories, fairy tales, songs, dances, herbal wisdom, and more that comprise the identity of a particular group of people from a geograph-ical area. These help to make up the cosmology, or worldview, of a people. They reveal what is meaningful and alive for a group and how they make meaning in their lives.

When we begin to research the cosmology of our peoples, we start to understand them more. We enter more deeply into conscious relationship with them.

You can enter a country into the Encyclopedia Mythica website and begin to peruse the various articles there. Read with the eyes of the heart, attuning to things that spark your imagination and stir your heart. Is there a symbol or story that especially resonates, even if you can't articulate why? Are there any synchronicities with your own life?

If there is a particular story that shimmers, try to go more deeply with that one piece. Or perhaps there is an aspect of the story that you feel a quickening in response to. Maybe there is a pear or a pomegranate in it, and you know this fruit is significant to the land of your ancestors. You can research what the layers of meaning here might be. These can begin to inform your understanding of your people and yourself. You might ask, what does this story have to say to me about who I am and what I cherish? What are the literal and mythic truths these stories embody? Mythic truths are not about fact but meaning. Myths help point us toward deeper meaning in the world beneath the surface of things.

So many of us are not indigenous to the land we live on. Our ancestors perhaps emigrated to find a better life or stole land to increase their wealth and opportunities. Many of us feel at root landless and homeless, adrift because we don't feel we belong where we are. When we don't have access to the stories of our ancestors as part of the place where we live, then we need to go searching for resources to help support that sense of homecoming and deep connection to the rituals and ways of understanding the world of our ancestors.

For those of us with ancestral lines stretching back to various European countries, we might find consolation in some of the words from Lyla June's essay "Reclaiming Our Indigenous European Roots." June is of Diné (Navajo), Tsétsêhéstâhese (Cheyenne), and European lineages living in New Mexico. She describes a spontaneous vision she had of her European grandmothers and grandfathers singing to her songs made of love in which they described a time before witch trials, crusades, and even the English language: "These grandmothers and grandfathers set the ancient medicine of Welsh bluestone upon my aching heart. Their chants danced like the flickering light of Tuscan cave-fires. Their joyous laughter echoed on and on like Baltic waves against Scandinavian shores. They blew worlds through my mind like windswept snow over Alpine Mountain crests. They showed to me the vast and beautiful world of Indigenous Europe. This precious world can scarcely be found in any literature but lives quietly within us like a dream we can't quite remember."[2]

This is an experience many of us long for, to connect with the ancient worlds of our lineages: to understand their worldviews, to participate in their rituals, and to sing their songs and tell their stories. For some of us these are lost to the cruelty of time and ancestors who left their countries and tried to fit into their new homelands, leaving behind their customs too. Or their ancestors were forcibly removed from their homelands the way the Africans of the slave trade were. Or the government tried to erase the memories of their languages and cultures, as with Indigenous Peoples/First Nations in the United States and Canada or even in Ireland with the occupation of British imperialist forces over hundreds of years.

We might experience grief over these losses, and that would be an appropriate response to the destruction of cultures over time. We might also desire to celebrate all the remnants that did persist, whether through story, song, food, or language. We might marvel at the enduring power of parts of a peoples' memory and what they fought to hold onto. Bringing these parts of ancestral culture back to life and integrated into our awareness is one way to bring healing to our family system as well.

LAIMA AND THE CUCKOO

Many years into my journey with working to heal my ancestral line, especially with my father, I was introduced to different kinds of ancestral lineage healing work. This process honors the reality that if we go far enough back in any of our cultural and genetic lines, we will eventually find cultures that had regular practices of connecting with the dead.

In this process you work in your imagination to slowly bring healing to each of your four main genetic lines: mother's mother, mother's father, father's father, and father's mother. An integral part of this process is connecting with a wise and well ancestor further back on the particular line you are working with, as they are the one to bring healing to the descendants that follow. You can do this process on your own or work with a trained guide. I found the guided process helpful, as it connected me with someone who holds the space for what unfolded. Over a period of a couple of years, I moved through those four genetic lines to bring healing. It is not an immediate process; it takes time to build relationships with ancient guides.

As I worked to heal my ancestral lines, I had also been doing a lot of genealogical research, even hiring some genealogists in the locations I was searching to get help finding family records. The first time I tried to trace my Latvian ancestors, I kept hitting a wall at my grandfather.

After healing my father's fatherline, I decided to try once more with research. Very soon after contacting the genealogist to help me, she sent me a message—"Christine, the Latvians are looking for you"—along with a link to an article online about my great-grandfather. I knew he had been a lawyer, but what I didn't know was that he was the first chief justice of the supreme court in the newly formed independent state after World War I. For their centenary celebration, they decided to honor his memory by planting an oak tree in the town of Kuldiga where he was from. The article ended by saying they were looking for his descendants.

I wrote an email to the address listed and received back an enthusiastic reply. Soon after, I was planning my next trip to Latvia. I continued to work with the genealogist, and she was able to trace back a couple more generations this time. John and I traveled to Latvia, first visiting Kuldiga to see the oak tree and visit the family cemetery that I had only recently discovered. Next to the cemetery was where the family home once stood, and we got to stand there in the remaining foundation and take in the view that would have nurtured them.

We then went on to Riga, where we were invited to the Supreme Court building and were greeted by the current chief justice. The woman guiding us had a binder full of research she had done on my great-grandfather's life, and she shared it with me. They had never been able to trace what happened to his children, as my grandfather fled Latvia with his wife and children (my father included) when the Russians invaded during World War II, and they never returned because of Soviet occupation.

As we were walking through the Supreme Court building, our host pointed out the statue of Lady Justice and mentioned her connection to the goddess Laima, who is known for determining people's fates in life. My ears perked up at hearing about her, as I am very interested in mythologies. When I got home, I searched online for more information about Laima. It turns out she is intimately connected with the cuckoo bird. Earlier, I shared about the cuckoo bird I encountered at my father's grave. Suddenly, my time at the cemetery three years prior had come full circle. At that moment, I felt the visitation was less about the cuckoo's trickster qualities and more about its connection to Laima and the destiny I was following to restore right relationship with my ancestors.

Whenever I think I have come to the end of my research, there is more to be discovered. I feel certain the healing work I did with my father's fatherline helped open up this rich vein of connection to his ancestors. The synchronicities of the cuckoo bird helped to give me a sense of confirmation that this was indeed some kind of communication from my father. Laima and the cuckoo continue to be important symbols for my personal journey, and they connect me intimately to my Latvian ancestors.

In this family systems work, every time I make a new discovery it leads me down a whole new trail of inquiry. Every question leads to a dozen more. Each thread I follow leads to a whole new landscape for exploration. It is exciting work and speaks to me of the complexity of who we are as human beings. Layer upon layer reveals an inexhaustible depth to our stories if we consider them rooted in the spiral of stories I spoke of earlier.

SONGS OF THE ANCESTORS AS GATEWAYS

When I lived in Seattle, I discovered there was a significant Latvian community there. They even had their own Lutheran church on the north end of the city. They also had a dance troupe that performed at various festivals and events. Latvian culture has an enormous body of folk songs, which are still preserved and sung today. Every five years in Riga, the capital of Latvia, there is a huge traditional song and dance festival in which thousands of singers and dancers come to perform. The lyrics of the songs contain clues to older ways of life, belief in the pre-Christian deities, practices of daily life, and relationships to nature.

Once I found out about the Seattle group, I started to attend their local performances. Inevitably during one of their songs I would begin to weep. I wasn't even sure of the source of my weeping, and I wouldn't have been able to name a specific cause. I didn't even understand the lyrics, as they were all in Latvian. But something about witnessing them embody this part of my ancestral heritage touched something wordless and unnameable in me. The songs felt like an act of healing and homecoming.

Listening to classical music has a similar effect on me. My father loved classical music and would often play it at home on our record player. Sometimes he'd play a Strauss Viennese waltz and invite me to dance in our small living room. While classical music doesn't have roots as deep in a culture as the Latvian folk song tradition does, it connects me to many generations of my Austrian grandmothers and grandfathers, for whom this music would have been a soundtrack to much of their lives.

Finding the music of our ancestors can become a powerful way to connect with them. Often music was used for prayer or celebrations, for lament, or to accompany daily tasks. When we reconnect to these songs, we can tap into a temple of sound that already exists inside of us. I will suggest later in the chapter that you learn one of these songs by looking up archives of folk songs from various countries.

We don't all connect to music in the same way, but these sounds can still evoke a sense of connection for us to ancestral landscapes and cultures. Even if we close our eyes and just listen and imagine our ancestors singing to us, this can be a powerful moment of intimacy and a different kind of knowing.

PRACTICE
Learning by Heart

Consider reclaiming the art of storytelling as a spiritual practice. You can tell stories from your own life or that of another person in your family. You can also learn a myth, folktale, or fairy tale from one of your ancestral lands and memorize the details.

Learning by heart was the primary way of knowing for most Indigenous cultures if we go far enough back in time. Oral tradition was how stories and memory were carried forward. In Ireland, knowing poems and stories by heart is still an important part of the culture. When I hear an Irish person share a poem they have memorized from one of their beloved poets, I witness the way the poems have become a part of them.

The Hebrew Scriptures have many passages that describe the new covenant as written not on stone but in the hearts of the people. These passages show a shift from a list of rules to follow to a true experience of conversion. The motivation to do good things in the world comes from an internal motivation rather than an external one. This speaks to me of the ripening wisdom of a people and how God speaks to us in different ways at different times. The beauty is that it says God is willing to try different approaches with us. We may need to hear the message in one form at a certain moment of our lives, but over time, it will come again to us in different ways. Each way is an opportunity for conversion, to make God's words a part of our lives.

The Irish monks would have sung the psalms throughout each day as a central part of their prayer. They were immersed in this poetry and ancient call to see God active in the whole world. When you speak and sing these words, you join in with these ancient prayers as well. They likely would have memorized all 150 of them as their days were so intertwined with their imagery.

Memorizing is a way of tending a sanctuary of memory within us. Find a story that shimmers for you and commit to learning it by heart. This doesn't necessarily mean word for word, as storytellers are forever embellishing their stories in new ways. It does mean contemplating the images, the unfolding of the narrative, and what it reveals to you about how your ancestors saw the world.

Often taking something—a story, a poem, a scripture—that you want to remember on a walk with you can be a helpful way of bringing the body into this practice. The story becomes embedded in our muscles and bones.

Another aspect of storytelling is to tell the stories of your mother or father, or your grandmothers and grandfathers. If there is a story you know, you could craft it into a tale to offer to others as a way of bringing voice to their experiences.

Randy Woodley describes how important it is in Indigenous cultures to honor, respect, and listen to elders. "We believe [elders] are approaching the crossover time, when they will walk on to the other world and come closer to the Great Mystery."[3] This is such a beautiful image. In Western culture, our elders are often shuffled off to nursing homes or dream of retirement and leisure. In addition, capitalism tells us growing older is to be avoided at all costs, and it tries to sell us products to prevent the inevitable aging we will experience. If you have elders who are still alive, consider inviting them to tell you a story about their lives. This can be an act of nurturing a deeper valuing of the gifts of aging and encouraging the practice of listening to elders and integrating the wisdom they offer.

Holocaust survivor and writer Elie Wiesel puts an even sharper point on this message of sharing the stories of elders and ancestors: "For the survivor who chooses to testify, it is clear: his duty is to bear witness for the dead and for the living. He has no right to deprive future generations of a past that belongs to our collective memory. To forget would be not only dangerous but offensive; to forget the dead would be akin to killing them a second time."[4] As I mentioned earlier, in Mexican culture there is a belief that everyone has another death when, after death, they are forgotten and their stories are no longer told. The celebration of Día de los Muertos is to make sure your loved ones are remembered for, as long as someone has a memory of them, they are never really gone.

MEDITATION
Lectio Divina with Myth or Folktale Excerpt

Find a myth, fairy tale, folktale, or other story from one of the cultures of your ancestors. Often you can find things easily by doing an online search at least as a starting place.

Once you find a story, spend some time reading it through to see if there is any resonance or dissonance or both within you. Pay attention especially to any sections, phrases, or words that shimmer for you. This means that it somehow calls to you and invites you to linger. Perhaps the story crafts an image that resonates deeply or stirs a memory.

Take this passage—I suggest you limit it to three to four sentences at most—and pray the ancient practice of lectio divina, or sacred reading, with it.

Allow a few moments to center yourself and bring yourself fully present. Bring your awareness down to your heart center, and invite in an open-hearted perspective, letting go of the need to think and figure things out.

Begin by reading through the passage you have selected at least twice slowly. As you read, listen for a word or phrase that shimmers forth for you, catches your attention, or calls to you in some way. Let this phrase echo in your heart or even repeat it gently aloud to hear the sound of it.

Then let the word or phrase unfold in your imagination, paying attention to images, feelings, and memories that arise and making space for whatever wants to come. Welcome in what your prayer brings to you.

Listen for the invitation you are hearing being offered to you in the word or phrase, and in the memories, feelings, and images of this prayer, with a text from your own lineage. Notice if there is a summons to some kind of new awareness or action. Allow time to hear between the thoughts as well. This isn't always a summons to some kind of doing but often an invitation into a different way of being. We are often called to change our perspective and how we interact with others rather than merely adding another thing to our to-do list.

Close your time by resting for a few minutes into the silence. Then spend some time journaling what you noticed or discovered.

CREATIVE EXPLORATION
Learn the Song of One of Your Ancestral Lands

I invite you to learn the song of one of your ancestral lands. The websites Folk Cloud (https://folkcloud.com) and Global Jukebox (https://theglobaljukebox.org) are both good places to get started. You can choose a region of the world and listen to various songs from those areas. It might be an instrumental piece of music or a song with lyrics. You could learn it on an instrument if you play one or learn to sing the words or hum the tune. Let this creative discovery be a meditative practice of connecting to your beloved dead. Feel them singing through your blood and bones, sparking the dance within you.

Blessing for Origins

This blessing comes as an ancient story
of how your people made sense of the world,

through famine, wars, plagues,
and times of abundance and celebration,
how they sang and danced
their cries, their joys, their sorrows.
Know these myths as your own,
look for what ties them to your own cherishing
and your sense of aliveness.
Let this blessing anchor you in meaning,
the kind that emerges over generations
of wrestling and loving,
the kind that still shimmers in us as dreams,
and when you awaken,
you know you've had a visitation.
Let the stories and songs
be a spiral path you can walk,
ancestral wisdom flowing forth
and deepening at every turn.
Learn these words, these tunes,
these movements by heart,
in your darkest hour let them return
to you like a summons and gift,
a map to guide you home again.

12

BECOMING A WISE AND WELL ANCESTOR

Maybe we dream new dreams just for ourselves. But, for certain, we also dream old dreams, recycle dreams dreamt by others who lived long before we were born. We appear to be eidetically similar to some of our ancestors in this way: Our ancestors' gifts and dreams did not die when their lives were cut away horrifically, or too soon, or even at the end of a long life.

—Clarissa Pinkola Estés, *Untie the Strong Woman*

Ultimately, these renewed and renewing connections to our blood and spiritual ancestors are in service of guiding us to live more fully. The great cloud of witnesses in the Letter to the Hebrews offers us inspiration and wisdom.

In light of our connection to our ancestors, being aware of the harm some of them caused, and embracing the blessing of those who are wise and well, there is one question we need to ask ourselves: how are we to live our own lives?

Our daily choices and actions have an effect on our immediate circles and also on the future. What we choose to validate by how we respond to life witnesses to a particular way of being, one that can support and reinforce others making similar choices. This is why community is so important for real spiritual growth and transformation. Living with integrity and love is challenging at times. We need others to walk alongside us with similar commitments. In the same way, the choices we make ripple out across space and time. Our actions encourage particular value systems and a vision for what the world is and can be.

We are alive because of our ancestors. They struggled, grieved, celebrated, and endured, and we can live our lives in ways that honor their memories. We can imagine that our ancestors would want their descendants to live good, fruitful, and meaningful lives. This is especially true for those ancestors who are wise and well and in loving relationship with us. They are allies for our creative unfolding and can offer guidance and wisdom. The more we work to heal the wounds we carry and those carried by our ancestors, the freer we become to live into the fullness we were created to experience.

Living in a loving, ethical way, aligned with our gifts and service to a world in need, is a profound way to honor the memory of our ancestors. As we bring what is unconscious to consciousness, learn to speak truth to others, release the hold of compulsions on our lives, and nourish our minds with education and our bodies through exquisite care, we are doing the hard work of fulfilling the ancestral birthright we carry. When we choose the path that is life-giving, rather than destructive to ourselves and others, we elevate their memory.

We are encouraged to remember and honor our ancestors through ritual and remembrance. Embodying their blessings in our lives is a most powerful way of honoring them as well.

DEDICATE LOVING ACTION

My maternal grandmother, Faith, was sadly a joyless and bitter woman. She died when I was twenty-four with my grandfather by her side, tending to all of her needs as pancreatic cancer ate away at her body. I spent a lot of time with my grandparents during the summers while growing up, and I don't ever remember seeing her smile. Before she got married, she had been a teacher, and she gave up that career to become a wife and mother of three children, the oldest of whom was my mother, and Faith eventually worked in my grandfather's business. Whenever she told stories of her days teaching, I sensed deep regret and great longing.

My paternal grandmother, Erika, I only met only once when I was six months old and my family flew to Vienna to be with her as she lay dying, also of pancreatic cancer. I have heard stories about her warmth and energy. Before she got married she was a dancer, a dream she also gave up for marriage and children and due to the necessities caused by living in Europe during both world wars.

Soon after starting this ancestral work, I became keenly aware of the profound limitations on my grandmothers' lives because of the era they lived in. Part of healing the wounds of the family line was to be in touch with their unfulfilled longings and desires. Slowly I began to see how my own work as teacher, writer, and artist was in a way an offering back to them. I could embody a freedom they were not able to. I often dedicate my work to their memory as a way of honoring what they endured in life, an endurance that helped bring me into existence.

During my journey toward healing these wounds, I became aware of how these different unfulfilled longings dwelled in me and competed for my energy; there is the writer/artist part of myself, the teacher part, the soul-care/spiritual director part, and the part that longs to work for justice. Of course, these are all woven together in the tapestry of my life. But it was a revelation to see how clearly my own calling is woven into the callings of my foremothers.

Alice Walker wrote, "And so our mothers and grandmothers have, more often than not anonymously, handed on the creative spark, the seed of the flower they themselves never hoped to see: or like a sealed letter they could not plainly read."[1] This was distinctly my experience; I feel as though I have been handed their creative sparks, which seeded my own passions in life.

They are an essential part of my cloud of witnesses, my Communion of Saints. And looking at calling in this context widens the horizons of the seed of who I am. When I craft my life to nurture my creativity, it is because I have the time, the means, and the support to do so. It is a privilege to be able to do so, one I do not take lightly. And yet, I too struggle with my own limits. I have chronic conditions that limit the amount I can do, and my creative energy often wants to extend far beyond my capacity to do so. Much of my journey has been learning to balance this longing with my own limits and living as fully as possible within my reality. I owe it to my foremothers. I owe it to myself. I owe it to the other women and men in my life whom I am blessed to encounter. This balancing is at the heart of crafting the sacred art of living.

Jungian analyst and storyteller Clarissa Pinkola Estés writes,

> Even though one generation passes from this earth, somehow many of each generation's hopes, ideas, and dreams seem to seek ground in generations following. Even if destroyed or buried, each generation's best ancestral ideas call to us across time, seeping up through the modern ground of our being like some inexhaustible artesian spring that undergirds our existence. . . . Whatever good we are seeking is also seeking us. Any good we have ever known in our family of human-kind, will find us again. The psyche is a universe unto itself in which nothing good is ever truly lost. Any lost or missing parts to the Holy, we will dream again. We will ever dream the Holy anew.[2]

The goodness we seek for our lives also seeks us. The passions we long to fulfill are calling out to us across generations to live into them as fully as we can. The dreams we have for ourselves are threaded through with the longings of our ancestors. If we could look back at the prior generations, we would see a beautiful tapestry of desire, both fulfilled and unfulfilled. It is up to us to weave into the tapestry the loose threads.

We can dedicate any positive and loving action to the memories of those who came before us. Whether you are living into the fullness of your calling, do work to support those in great need, or simply live as ethically as you can, all of these actions are embodying your ancestral connections. You can offer your actions to them. You are already an extension of their beingness in body and spirit, so your actions will inevitably ripple back to them. Making it conscious and intentional helps to amplify the impact. You can dedicate the action to the ancestors in general or focus on someone specific for particular actions, the way I do with my grandmothers and my livelihood through teaching and creative work. This can be a part of the healing work we extend back through the generations.

I teach about spiritual practice as a way that we embody our values. The way we live bears witness to an alternative way of being. One reason I am so drawn to contemplative life is that I believe it is such a nourishing antidote to the capitalist consumer culture we live in, which tries to extract every last ounce of energy we have in service to some larger machine where others profit at our expense and at the expense of the earth.

In an essay titled "Nourishing," Rowen White offers this beautiful insight:

> In our Mohawk stories, our elders tell us our life here on Earth is a gestation, a reproductive cycle that mirrors the life cycles happening all around us. At our birth, we are sprouting all of our ancestors' wildest dreams, at death we are a sowing of all that we pray and hope for our future generations. While we are alive and walking this pathway of life, we are continually reminded in our ceremonies and stories about the importance of the cultural seeds we can grow and incubate in our lives, in the grand hope that much more life will sprout from our graves and our memory when we become ancestors.[3]

When we arrive into this life and world, we bring the great dreams of our ancestors. As we navigate through life, we bring to fulfillment, as much as possible, those dreams. When we approach death, we offer those dreams to future generations as the seeds Alice Walker wrote about.

We can see this reality in both our blood ancestors and our spiritual ones. If we follow the Christian tradition, we can see Jesus as the fulfillment of all that came before him. Every generation that follows is called to live out the dream that Jesus proclaimed, a world where all those on the margins are welcome into the center, a place where we visit those in prison, care for the sick, and feed the hungry. We embody those dreams as much as we can, and we leave them as a legacy for those who follow.

In *Another Way: Living and Leading Change on Purpose*, Stephen Lewis writes about the Gospel of Luke containing Jesus's genealogy.

> What was the work that Jesus began? The work began with Jesus exhuming and retrieving fragmented, genealogical stories of his ancestors. The genealogy is a list of names that may not mean much to the reader of Scripture other than to authenticate Jesus's messianic role. Similar to the list of names of our own family trees, names signify so much more to the descendants and family historian. They represent stories of our ancestors and memories about who they were, their faith, and how they overcame in the face of struggle and uncertainty. Our family genealogies reveal to us stories about our people—from whom and where we come, their hopes and dreams and their contributions. More importantly, genealogies remind us that we were born into an ancestral lineage and we take our rightful place alongside heroes and heroines, queens and kings, freedom fighters and warrior-healers, god-bearers and prophets, dispossessed and possessed mothers and fathers who came before us and on whose shoulders we stand. If you want to understand Jesus and his purpose you must understand the lineage from which he emerged. . . . Remembering and reclaiming the ancient knowledge, power, pride, authority, and legacy of his people fueled his public service on behalf of the dispossessed. It fueled his resolve and resiliency in moments of temptation and tribulation.[4]

This is a beautiful way to imagine Jesus's sense of calling in his life as profoundly connected to his lineage in the same way that ours is. We carry on the work of our ancestors and our spiritual teachers. Our calling in life is not the individual call of a single lifetime, but one that ripples across the generations. Our ancestors listened to their own callings to build a better world and we benefit from their generosity of spirit. The more we can honor this legacy consciously, the more the blessings will flow from our actions.

Cultural Wounds and Repair

Similarly, if we discover in our family trees that our ancestors were slaveholders, were involved with the genocide of Indigenous Peoples, or other similar atrocities, we can also do intentional work to help transmute the effects of these violent disruptions to community and love. For example, my great-great-grandfather abused his wife to such an extent that she sought and was granted a divorce, which was both quite scandalous and hard to do in the late 1800s. I can donate money to a women's shelter in acknowledgment of this truth in my family line and as a way to help bring healing and restitution to what he did. I can dedicate conscious loving relationships to help restore this disruption to love.

In the fall of 2019, I traveled to the Northeast United States to teach, and I stayed in the area for an extra week to visit family and seek out about a dozen cemeteries in Massachusetts that hold the remains of many of my ancestors. I can trace one family line back to the *Mayflower*, meaning that part of my family arrived early on as settlers and colonizers. A couple of the cemeteries indicated that there were also older Indigenous burial grounds at the same spot, and I had to wonder how my ancestors' burials worked to erase the existence of that burial ground. Even though my life in Ireland feels far removed from this reality of early colonization, I can dedicate loving action to help repair these wounds specifically. This might be again through the donation of financial resources to organizations that help to lift up the lives of Indigenous peoples or, if I were living in the United States, it might be a form of direct connection with these communities to offer my service in whatever way is needed.

This work of intentional repair is an invitation to examine your own power, privilege, and complicity in unequal and unjust systems and take responsibility for helping to bring things to more harmony and peace.

In his powerful book *The Purpose Gap*, theologian Patrick B. Reyes describes the gap that people experience in education, wealth, housing, and opportunity, which also leads to a gap in being able to fulfill their purpose. Books about finding one's purpose are written for those who have the resources available to them to follow these calls. For others, the opportunity to live fully into their calling is stolen from them through inequality. "Closing the purpose gap means creating the conditions for future generations to achieve meaningful and purpose-filled lives. It means removing the barriers, generating the resources, building the power, and imagining the future where those who are most marginalized thrive. It is spirit work."[5] This is another way we can bring repair and healing to the cultural impacts of our ancestors' actions. We can choose a particular way of addressing these inequalities, work to help resolve the issue, and dedicate our work as an offering to our ancestors.

The healing of wounds is not just to heal individual ancestors but also to help heal the impact their lives had on others, which ripples across time as well. This honoring of our ancestors and making reparations for the harm they committed is in service to the collective. It opens the pathway of love to flow more freely between generations. It also calls us to consider the effect our actions will have on future generations, and it invites us to leave a legacy of love, as much as we are able.

COMING HOME TO WHERE YOU LIVE

Winona LaDuke, an activist of Ojibwe and Jewish descent, describes the work we've been doing as "intergenerational accountability" and asks, "How do I account my behaviors and decisions to my ancestors and to my descendants?" She goes on to counsel to make the place you live your home. Learn the names of its creatures and plant life; defend and protect its waters. "Keep that covenant, that agreement that we will take care of what is given to us, and your descendants will be grateful."[6]

You may not be able to return to the land of your ancestors for any number of practical reasons. This may not even be desirable, given that many of us are descended from a variety of cultures. My British and New England ancestors come from a very different culture than my Latvian, Czech, Austrian, and Slovenian ancestors. I can visit these places to feel an embodied connection and sense of homecoming. But then I return to Ireland, a place I love as well. John's maternal ancestors come from this place, but mine do not. Regardless of my ancestral connection to this land, I am called, by virtue of living here, to be a loving guardian of the place. The longer I live here, the more I learn about the geology, botany, marine biology, mythology, and spirituality of this place and its ancestors. Each time I learn a word in the Irish language, I feel slightly more connected to the story that is unfolding here. I root myself more deeply.

Randy Woodley, a Cherokee writer and theologian, invites us to consider the following: "We are all indigenous to some place. . . . Your ancestors were, at one time, all indigenous. . . . Your parents, grandparents, and great-grandparents who loved and breathed and experienced life before you—they are now living through you. From manifold generations back, they looked forward, sometimes even on their deathbeds, to your life. They and their indigeneity matter because you are here now as their living hope."[7] This is a very powerful awareness and antidote to what seems to be the profound disconnect those of us who are White colonizers with settler ancestors have to the land they have stolen. He also encourages us to regain this ancestral indigeneity by becoming rooted in the land that sustains us.

Dr. Leny Strobel is a professor of American multicultural studies at Sonoma State University and cofounder of a nonprofit organization that facilitates the process of decolonization and re-indigenization, specifically among Filipinos in the diaspora. In an interview about the wisdom of Martín Prechtel, a shaman living in New Mexico, she said that he was writing about building a house of origins, saying that when you build a home, you must make sure that everything in your house holds stories that you want to pass on to your children or future generations.

Strobel took this invitation seriously and began creating altars in her home, including an ancestral altar, an altar made of pictures of her family, another of objects she brought back from the Philippines, and another altar of her husband's objects that he brought from where he had come from in eastern Montana. "They became the bearers of stories. This makes dwelling very meaningful for me."[8]

There are many layers to this important work of coming home—from becoming more intimate with the land we live on and the creatures and plants that grow and thrive there to learning the stories the original peoples would tell. Then there is the work within our homes of creating a meaning-filled space, which is an antidote to the mindless consumerism so many of us engage in without considering the consequences, in terms of both the enormous amounts of waste and the disconnection we feel from our lives because we are so rarely surrounded by anything local, handmade, or ancestral. The intentional ways we choose to connect with the past and adorn our living spaces are all dimensions of becoming wise and well ancestors ourselves. We are called to be at home wherever we live, and we are called to become intimate with the stories and landscape our ancestors held dear. We are called to hold both in open palms.

One last word about descendants. You may be someone, like me, who has no children of your own. Or perhaps your children have passed away before you. Regardless, we can consider our descendants the generations that will follow us whether or not we are related by blood. This work teaches us that we still have responsibility for what comes next for the future world we help to build. We hold a sacred duty to future humans, animals, plants, and other living beings to bring love, equality, peace, and security to all.

PRACTICE
Remember You Will One Day Die

In the Christian monastic tradition starting with the Desert Mothers and Fathers, we find the practice of *memento mori*, remembering daily that you will one day die. We live in a culture terrified of growing older, of losing our abilities, and ultimately, of death. We are marketed all kinds of products to restore our youthfulness.

But mortality can be a gift when it leads us to cherish our lives even more. When we awaken each day and remember that this is grace, that our lives are freely given to us, we might be able to savor the goodness of each moment with more depth and delight. When we realize that our time is limited, we recognize that we need to make choices about what to embrace and what to release. We can imagine ourselves on our deathbeds and pray about what our regrets might be. I doubt many of us would regret not spending more time on the computer, but we likely would regret not making more time for loved ones.

My years of work with my ancestors—getting to know them, making time each day to honor their memory, conversing with them, traveling to the places where they lived and loved, and visiting the gravesites where they are buried—reinforce three things for me. First is that the dead are a loving communion, longing to be in relationship with us and ready to offer the wisdom of living through life's challenges. Second, my own death, rather than a fearful thing, might become an act of coming home to the love of these thousands who celebrate me and my life and what I have become. They await me with open arms. And third, my life matters. St. Benedict wrote that we are to "keep death daily before [our] eyes" (*The Rule of St. Benedict*, 4:47). This awareness of my mortality each day can become a summons to remembering my calling in life. I may feel like a tiny drop in an enormous sea, but my actions are important and contribute to the cultivation of love in the world. This practice asks me to consider regularly what I want my legacy to be. It reminds me that time is fleeting and precious.

I hope to live a very long time because, despite the heartbreak, each day also brings sweetness and great beauty. But I do take comfort knowing I have reached out in heartfelt earnestness to bridge the gap between worlds. Honoring my ancestors means I am also preparing for a good death, one where I don't think I will have regrets, one that reflects a beautiful life of loving those closest to me as well as the wider community of past, present, and future.

MEDITATION
Connecting with Ancestral Lines

Prepare yourself for meditation time by slowing down your breath and moving into a comfortable position. Gently ease your mind and soften your brow; let your awareness drop into your heart as you enter consciously into your inner sanctuary. Here you are met by the perpetual presence of the divine spark that burns within each person. Open your arms in a gesture of openness and gratitude and rest for a few moments into the grace of being.

Ask for a circle of protection to be drawn around you so that nothing that wishes you harm can penetrate this shield of light. Call in any angels, saints, or guides who can help fortify this protection for you and be present with you.

Imagine that you are shown a doorway from inside the sanctuary of the heart. You are being invited to cross this threshold, but you must first connect with a deep question of the heart. Allow a few moments to reflect on where you are in your life right now and what wisdom you are seeking to move into this next season. See if a question arises for you, perhaps something you would love some clarity about. What arises could even be as simple as how to live well so that when death comes you will be able to transition with greater peace.

As you look through the doorway, you see a beautiful meadow under evening light. The breezes blow gently, and everything is in bloom. You remove your shoes because you know this is holy ground and step through. You feel the soft grass under your feet as you stand under a sacred tree in this meadow. You need to walk only a few yards to reach the center of the meadow where the moonlight is shimmering.

Standing in the center of the meadow under the glow of the moon, suddenly you see four lines of people extending in each of the four cardinal directions. One line is your mother's motherline, and you see your maternal grandmother and all of her mothers and grandmothers standing behind her in a long line that extends farther than you can see. Another line is your mother's fatherline, and you see your maternal grandfather and all his fathers and grandfathers extending back. The third line is your father's fatherline, and you see your paternal grandfather and all of his fathers and grandfathers extending back through space and time. And finally, the fourth line is your father's motherline, and you see your paternal grandmother and all of her mothers and grandmothers behind her. Even if you did not know your parents or grandparents, hold space open for the possibility of a loving connection through the veil.

Stand in the center for a few moments, feeling the grace of being surrounded by your ancestors, the great cloud of witnesses. You know that there are some gathered here who still need healing beyond the veil, but you also know there are many thousands more who swim in the most profound love and are here to extend that loving grace and healing to you and the world.

Call to mind and heart the question you are holding. You begin with your mother's motherline. A wise and well representative from this line steps forward and offers her blessing on you and a word of wisdom that you receive.

Turn to your mother's fatherline, and a wise and well father from this line steps forward and offers his blessing on you and some wisdom to carry with you.

Turn to your father's fatherline; a wise and well one from this line comes forward and offers his blessing and a response to your question.

Finally, turn to your father's motherline, and a wise and well mother from this line walks toward you; she places her hands in blessing on you and offers her wisdom to you.

Once you have received a blessing from all four lines and their words of wisdom, you stand for a moment there in the center savoring this gift. You look around, seeing them all there, and you know in this moment that they are always present for you; you just need to call upon them.

When the time comes to leave, you offer a gesture of gratitude in each direction. Then step through the portal back to the sanctuary of your heart. Breathe here for a few moments, and then slowly and gently return to the room. Spend some time noting down anything that felt important.

CREATIVE EXPLORATION
Stories of Redemption

InterPlay,[9] founded by Cynthia Winton Henry and Phil Porter, is an amazing community and set of improvisational practices to cultivate creativity and connection. One of the practices is to tell what is called a "story of redemption." This is when we retell a story from our lives that carries pain and wounding, such as a family dysfunction or an early loss that perhaps makes us feel stuck. In the traditional form, the person would tell a life event, imagining it as they wish it could have been and telling the story as if it had been so. In this way, the person gives themselves the emotional gift of having that which they long for and inviting in the healing God desires for them. For example, you might recall a mistake you made that led to you hurting someone else. In your retelling you can imagine that instead of the relationship fracturing, you reached out for forgiveness and received kindness and understanding. You can explore this practice first in its original form.

I suggest another step with this. Imagine a story from your ancestral line. Perhaps it is the wounding your mother or father experienced in childhood. Name something you know to be true. This might come from research of significant events that impacted the culture like war, widespread illness, crop failures, or financial devastation. Then see the story unfolding across generations. Imagine the healing that might come when you offer your own loving actions in the world. Tell the story of redemption in which the pain or rupture that happened in one generation is then healed by the actions in a later generation, honoring that we are part of one long ancestral body.

Blessing for Becoming Wise and Well

We dream the dreams of old,
the longings of our ancestors
arising in the surrender of the night.
Each choice we make to love,

each moment of kindness ripples across time,
each speaking of truth brings integrity,
each moment we live into a new way of being
and witness to something different as possible,
we become the world we want to see,
we carry forward the desires of the ancients
for peace and ease and joy.
This blessing comes as a call,
to release the hold of old compulsions
and what depletes and destroys,
to nourish yourself with exquisite care,
a reminder that the ancestors ache for this,
to bring your ancient birthright into fullness.
May the grandmothers and grandfathers
bless you with clarity and alignment
to bring your gifts in service
to a torn and trembling world.
To do these things with intention
is to elevate their memory with honor.
This blessing comes as a dedication,
for love to disrupt all the wounded patterns,
for you to remember where you came from,
but also the place you are
and who you are becoming.
Learn the names of trees and stones,
of flowers and birdsong.
Be a loving guardian of the land beneath your feet,
let your home become a bearer of stories
to leave for the future waiting to be born.

13

ANCESTRAL EARTH AND DEEP TIME

Each time my feet touched the earth I knew my mother was there with me. I knew this body was not mine alone but a living continuation of my mother and my father and my grandparents and great-grandparents. Of all my ancestors. These feet that I saw as "my" feet were actually "our" feet. Together my mother and I were leaving footprints in the damp soil.

From that moment on, the idea that I had lost my mother no longer existed. All I had to do was look at the palm of my hand, feel the breeze on my face or the earth under my feet to remember that my mother is always with me, available at any time. . . . Pay attention to all the leaves, the flowers, the birds, and the dewdrops. If you can stop and look deeply, you will be able to recognize your beloved one manifesting again and again in many forms.

—Thich Nhat Hanh, *No Death, No Fear*

We have been exploring our ancestral connections to our human ancestors, but I invite you to turn your attention to an even deeper look at time and connection to the universe. Earth is our ancestor too, as well as the stars. We contain elements of these in our body and blood. If we could trace our ancestral lineage back far enough, we would reach the limits of our human existence and then travel back into the previous evolutions of being that we have moved through, all the way back to the origins of our planet and even the solar system and galaxy.

I invite you to consider your ancestral connection to Earth and your kin as being made up of all of Earth's beings and creatures. We know through the science of evolution that we are the development of millions of years of unfolding and adapting. If we could trace our lineage back far enough, we would discover it winding through all manner of animal beings. In addition, the rootedness and belonging of our ancestors to particular places in the world means that we can call on the rivers, seas, and mountains as our ancestors as well.

Many of us will find connection to our human ancestors through a relationship with nature. I know after my mother died butterflies started appearing in different ways and became a sign to me of her presence. After my aunt Nancy, my mother's sister, died, I went for a long walk in the woods to find some consolation and was met by two butterflies flittering alongside each other and following me up the trail for a long while. I smiled at the presence of my mother and my aunt there with me. I feel my ancestors' presence in the strength and resilience of trees. The river becomes a sign of the flow of life through generations.

We may find our loved ones in the signs and symbols of nature, but these Earth elements have also shaped the imaginations of our ancestors. Writer Sharon Blackie explores the idea of "psychogeology," how the geologic foundations of where we live affect our psyches. She describes living on the Isle of Lewis in western Scotland:

> Metamorphic rock—yes, metamorphic: a word shot through with all the possibilities of transformation that I could ever want. How could such a place not define me? It changes in form, it adapts to whatever storms and stresses may come along. It is phoenix rock, emerging renewed from temperatures greater than 1,500 degrees Celsius and pressure

that is greater than 1,500 bars. Such things of necessity cause
profound change if you mean to survive them. More than
simply transformed, this rock has endured, and there are times
in everyone's life when endurance matters.[1]

Just as the stone where we live can affect how we experience and
understand the world, so has it shaped our ancestors and their ways of
being.

In her essay "Moving with the Rhythms of Life," Katherine Kassouf
Cummings writes about the French word *depaysement*, which describes
someone who is out of place and "expresses the disorientation of being
away from one's homeland, acknowledging the connection between
well-being and belonging to a particular place." She goes on to write,
"Each of us can trace our lives, through generations, to this original
kinship. Though we may not know their names, we all have ancestors
who knew the lands and waters as their relations, and we all have
ancestors in the land. *Depaysement* rests in our bodies. We long to
belong."[2] This primal sense of home and belonging is something we all
carry within us whether we are conscious of those forces at work or not.

One of the things that I marveled at the most when we moved
to Ireland was the geology. It was something I had never really paid
attention to before in the previous places I lived. But living in Galway
city, in the west of Ireland at the confluence of two distinct geological
regions—the limestone landscape of the Burren and the granite
landscape of Connemara—brought the qualities of stone alive to me
in a new way.

The Burren, to the south, is a region known for its karst landscape,
which means the bedrock is exposed. When you visit, it looks almost
as if you've landed on the moon with its soft gray stone hills. The
limestone that makes up this area is actually tropical seabed from 330
million years prior, when sea creatures essentially were compressed
into stone and the geological shelf drifted over time from the equator to
where Ireland is now at the fifty-fourth latitude. These stones literally
embody the ancestors, some of the very earliest forms of life on Earth.
It is a marvel to walk across this stone and imagine it contains the fossils
of primeval sea life. Limestone is soft, so there are rounded edges and

holes where the water has worn through. Lakes called *turloughs* develop beneath the stone and are only visible in winter when water levels rise.

Connemara, to the west, is very different; it is granite landscape and even more ancient at 470 million years old and formed from volcanic flow. Granite is hard, so the edges and mountains are sharper and more jagged and rough looking than in the Burren. Water does not penetrate below the rock, so it is a region rich with lakes across the surface.

Anyone who has been to Ireland will likely be familiar with all the stone walls that you see surrounding green fields. This was a way farmers could mark their boundaries, keep their sheep and cattle contained, and clear their fields of stone so that the livestock could feed. There is also an abundance of stone ruins dotting the landscape— megalithic passage tombs, stone circles, ancient forts, and hundreds of church ruins. You can find threshold stones at various sacred sites in the landscape. These are markers of the doorway from one world to another. Stone has been a significant part of the religious imagination here for as long as humans have inhabited the land. When you visit these sites, it is clear that if you slow down and listen closely you can hear the whispers of the stones. You can imagine the thousands of pilgrims who would have prayed at the tombs, in the circles, or in the church structures, each bringing their own longing and the stone carrying it for them. In these places, you can feel a connection with other pilgrims and with the great cloud of witnesses.

You might be, like me, an avid collector of stones when you visit a place. There is a primal desire to connect to these mineral beings and their density of substance, how they speak of solidity and ancientness. Some people seek heart-shaped stones, some only round and smooth stones. I am drawn to stones that look like eggs, a reminder of the new life and possibility they hold.

Thomas Merton wrote in *New Seeds of Contemplation*, "The great, gashed, half-naked mountain is another of God's saints. There is no other like him. He is alone in his own character; nothing else in the world ever did or ever will imitate God in quite the same way. That is his sanctity."[3]

When I lived in Seattle, on sunny days Mount Rainier hovered in the sky like magic, invisible most days in the mist and fog. It was a sacred mountain to the original settlers of that land, as so many of the mountains in the world are. Mountains have always been places of theophany—an encounter with holiness—such as Moses at Mount Sinai, where he received God's laws and saw God's face. Mount Tabor in Israel is where Jesus became transfigured before his disciples.

There are more references to mountains and hills in the Bible than to any other geographical feature. Noah's ark came to rest on a mountain, God tested Abraham on a mountain, and Moses received the Ten Commandments on a mountain. Jesus went to a mountain to pray, the Mount of Olives, before his crucifixion on a hill. Mountains stretch our imaginations upward in celebration of a transcendent God who creates with glory and majesty.

In the fifth century, St. Patrick went up the sacred mountain, now called Croagh Patrick, and fasted at the summit for forty days. It is now known as Ireland's pilgrimage mountain because more than a million people each year come to climb it and connect with the longing for God that carried St. Patrick to its summit.

Even the stones are our ancestors. Their minerals strengthen our bones. Their heights inspire our imaginations.

Deep Time

Seeing Earth as our ancestor invites us into a deeply interconnected way of seeing and experiencing our relationship to the world and to time. Deep time is geologic time, time from the perspective of stone, the formation of mountains, and planetary movements of tectonic plates. Geologist Marcia Bjornerud writes in her book *Timefulness*, "Fathoming deep time is arguably geology's single greatest contribution to humanity. Just as the microscope and telescope extended our vision into spatial realms once too minuscule or immense for us to see, geology provides a lens through which we can witness time in a way that transcends the limits of our human experience."[4] It may be an awe-inspiring thought to consider how you are part of a lineage of thousands of generations of human ancestors. How much more wondrous to consider how this lineage extends even further back through time.

Catholic priest and theologian Thomas Berry believed that the future of humanity rests not in scientific discovery or political systems but in our capacity to cultivate "intimate communion" with Earth.[5] This will be a development that demands new cultural forms where we can become fully present to the numinous alive in the world around us. He locates the guidance we need in our very genes: "We must find our primary source of guidance in our genetic coding. These tendencies are derived from the larger community of the Earth and eventually from the universe itself. In Jungian terms, these tendencies identify with those psychic energy constellations that take shape as the primary archetypal forms deep in the unconscious realms of the human."[6] He goes on to write that how we understand ourselves and our identity and calling "must begin where the universe begins. Not only does our physical shaping and spiritual perception begin with the origin of the universe, so too does the formation of every being in the universe."[7]

Astrophysicist Karel Schrijver and his wife, Iris, a medical doctor specializing in genetics, write in their book *Living with the Stars* about how our bodies are quite literally made of stardust:

> Our bodies are made of the burned-out embers of stars that were released into the Galaxy in massive explosions long before gravity pulled them together to form the Earth. These remnants now comprise essentially all the material in our bodies. Most of it has been cycling through the continents, with a small amount added only recently, when comets were captured by the Earth's gravity, or when ultrafast particles ran into the atmosphere and created a shower of new particles. It is being used by all living beings on the planet. Plants capture sunlight and release oxygen even as they create food for us, humans. We live by the grace of stardust assembled by plants into nutrients that provide us with energy to grow, to move, and to think.[8]

The cosmos is our most ancient ancestor, swimming through our blood and strengthening our bones. We are connected to all of life through this common genetic inheritance of stardust. We are all made of the same substance.

They go on to write, "We are, indeed, stardust, in a very literal sense. Every object in the wider universe, everything around us, and everything we are, originated from stardust. Thus, we are not merely connected to the universe in some distant sense: stardust from the universe is actually flowing through us on a daily basis, and it rebuilds the stars and planets throughout the universe as much as it does our bodies, over and over again."[9]

Writer Sophie Strand has a beautiful reflection on what it means to connect to Earth as an ancestor:

> Every one of your cells holds an ancient and anarchic love story. Around 2.7 billion years ago free-living prokaryotes melted into one another to form the mitochondria and organelles of the cells that build our bodies today. . . . If you live in a valley, chances are the ancient glacial moraine, the fossils crushed underfoot, the spores from grandmotherly honey fungi, have all entered into and rebuilt the very molecular make up of your bones, your lungs, and even your eyes. . . . Your body is an ecosystem of ancestors. An outcome born not of a single human thread, but a web of relations that ripples outwards into the intimate ocean of deep time.[10]

This expansive perspective calls us to widen our view of what has made us and formed us in this physical realm. Imagine that you are created from the very stuff of creation around you: ancient stone forming your bones, wild plants nourishing your body, and springs of water flowing through your veins.

BREATH OF LIFE

As inhabitants of planet Earth, we all breathe the same air. This sea of oxygen and carbon dioxide, among other gases, is like a sea of life. It sustains us. What we exhale, the plants take in and convert to oxygen so that we can inhale again. If we reflect on this reality, we see how profoundly breath and air connect us not only to one another as human beings but also to the creatures who breathe and the plant life that does a dance with us to keep the air life-giving for us.

There is another gas we breathe in and out with each breath called argon, which is an inert gas. This means it does not interact with any other elements. The very same argon molecules that existed hundreds of thousands of years ago still permeate the air that we breathe today. They remain unchanged because they don't react with other substances. Argon comprises about 1 percent of each breath.

With each breath, we breathe the air that St. Francis of Assisi and Napoleon breathed. We breathe the air that the poet Mary Oliver breathed, that Nelson Mandela breathed, that King Tutankhamun breathed, and that the ancient Israelites breathed. We breathe the air that Mary and Jesus breathed. And perhaps even more vital to the work we've been doing, we are breathing the air our ancestors breathed as well. We are connected to our grandparents and great-grandparents and back through the generations through the simple act of inhalation and exhalation. We are breathing the same argon particles that they did. Our breath creates a thread of connection that is deep and wide.

While this may not have the same sense of physical substance as the stardust we are made of, it is a remarkable reality that the air we breathe as part of our survival connects us both across space on the planet and across time back through millions of generations of humans and other life forms.

PRACTICE
Earth as Our Original Monastery

You may be familiar with one of my earlier books, *Earth, Our Original Monastery: Cultivating Wonder and Gratitude through Intimacy with Nature*.[11] In that book, I describe the ways Earth serves as our primary and original sanctuary space by drawing on scriptures, saints, spiritual directors, icon, sacraments, and liturgy. Threaded throughout the sacred texts of the Jewish and Christian traditions are celebrations of the ways Earth is a wisdom teacher and guide for us.

One thing I suggest frequently in that book is a practice called a contemplative walk, which is a walk where you aren't trying to get anywhere; you show up in full presence to the world around you. It is a practice of encounter, of opening our hearts to hear what nature and the world have to say to us through the sounds of wind, the colors of a flower, the swooping of birds, the rustle of leaves, the shape of a tree, and the shimmering of a stone.

Each time something makes you want to pause, you rest and receive, you open your heart to wonder, and you listen for the wisdom being offered without trying to figure anything out. You let your heart be moved by the world. You enter into a relationship of mutuality with all of creation and encounter it as a beloved ancestor. Consider, as you take this walk, what Earth might be trying to teach you. Open your heart to receive it.

MEDITATION
Ancestral Earth

Begin with a few moments of centering, allowing your body to soften and your mind to arrive as fully to the present moment as you can. Deepen your breath, and with each inhale, imagine calling in the presence of the Spirit, the Great Breath who breathed all life into being from the very first moment of creation. With every exhale, soften and release anything you are holding onto as much as possible.

Let your breath direct your attention from your mind and thoughts down into your body, coming to rest in your heart center. Breathe there for a few moments, connecting to the infinite Source of Compassion, the one who shaped our bodies out of the clay of the earth. Feel yourself held in this moment, without the need to do anything, and simply allow yourself to be.

Bring your attention back to your breath, and as you inhale and exhale, call to mind those argon molecules that travel in and out with every breath, the ones that have existed unchanged throughout time. Imagine with each breath that you are connecting to all the other humans on this planet who are also breathing. Then widen out to the animals and other breathing creatures. Then out to the plant life that sustains you.

Then shift your view back across time, and as you breathe, see your ancestors breathing with you. Imagine the life breath that sustained the generations of grandparents and great-grandparents back through time. See the breath of life sustaining them and you in a great circle. Then widen out your view and imagine the way your breath connects you to all the other humans who have lived and the creatures breathing the same air.

Then turn your attention to your physical body with its skin, muscles, tendons, and bones. Become aware that you are made up of stardust, and in your imagination, visualize the way stardust comprises all of life on Earth now and back through time. Spend some time again specifically focusing on your ancestors. See your lineages shimmering with stardust back through thousands of years. Reach back to before your first human ancestor existed, and see the life forms that contributed to who you are and who your ancestors developed into. Imagine them shimmering with stardust.

Continue back in your imagination all the way to that original explosion of fire and light that brought everything into existence. Feel yourself connected to this primordial event in a very intimate and physical way. You might even make a physical connection with your body, massaging your arms and legs, feeling the solidity of your body in this moment and honoring the stardust that has created you, that is in your genes, as it made up the bodies of all those who walked this Earth before you.

Rest in this expansive, loving awareness for as long as you need. Then slowly and gently return your awareness back to this moment in time, back to your body here and now. Allow a few slow, deep breaths to anchor yourself back in the present moment and then gently return to the room.

CREATIVE EXPLORATION
Ancestor Stones

In Jewish tradition, as we read earlier, stones can become sacred objects to help us remember our connection between the worlds of the visible and invisible. We first read of a stone as a doorway in Genesis 28:10–22, when Jacob is on a long journey and lies down to rest with his head on a stone as a pillow. He crosses a threshold into the dreamworld and sees the ladder of angels ascending and descending. When he awakens, he takes the stone and sets it up as a pillar, pouring oil on it and calling it House of God.

Consider creating some ancestor stones. In the winter of 1955–1956, Carl Jung chiseled the names of his paternal ancestors on three stone tablets and placed them in the courtyard of his home. "When I was working on the stone tablets," he wrote, "I became aware of the fateful links between me and my ancestors."[12] Consider going on a walk in the woods or on the beach and gather stones together. Bring them home and draw with either permanent marker or paint the names of your ancestors onto each stone and place them in your altar space. You could also add the names of animal beings you feel a connection to or the name of the lands your lineage is rooted in to honor that deeper ancestral Earth connection. Make some time to hold each of them in your hands, make space within yourself to receive their gifts and wisdom, and reflect on the journeys of the people whose stories are so much a part of your own.

A Blessing for Deep Time

This blessing shimmers across the ages,
from the ancestors of stone and stars
there is a sacred thread connecting us
to the first moments of everything.
Millions of years
of unfolding, shaping, emerging, adapting,

you are made from the embers of galaxies.
Limestone holds remains of ancient seabeds,
fossils embedded in stones beneath us.
You are part of the Earth lineage,
your body an ecosystem of ancestors
forming a web of ancient life.
See your loved ones
still speak in leaf and loam,
in gills and granite,
in water and on the uplift of wings.
This blessing is an anchor in eternity,
in the ancient wisdom arising
from everything that is alive,
primordial fire pulsing through us,
the origin of love.

CONCLUSION: THE LOVE OF THOUSANDS

Nothing is more practical than finding God, that is, than falling in a love in a quite absolute, final way. What you are in love with, what seizes your imagination will affect everything. It will decide what will get you out of bed in the mornings, what you will do with your evenings, how you spend your weekends, what you read, who you know, what breaks your heart, and what amazes you with joy and gratitude. Fall in love, stay in love, and it will decide everything.

—Joseph Whelan, SJ

We have been journeying throughout this book to connect across the veil to the invisible world where angels, saints, and ancestors dwell. The mystics remind us that this world is not far away but right in front of us if we only have eyes to see. Honoring the saints and ancestors in particular is not a morbid act of revering death but a way of practicing resurrection. It is a celebration of the many layers of love and support we have available to us if we just attune ourselves to that love.

The story of Easter morning in John 20 is such a story of surprise and complete reversal of expectation. Two of the disciples and Mary

Magdalene go very early to the tomb only to discover Jesus's body is missing. They are deep in grief, then confused, and even angry that the body has been moved. Like all threshold moments of our lives, there is a powerful call here. Where you expect to find death, you suddenly discover the evidence of death is gone. Where you expect to discover the broken body in the tomb, you encounter one who has been transformed, but you do not recognize it right away. Perhaps you have even had a few moments like this as we traveled through our growing friendship with angels, saints, and ancestors, moments of holy surprise. You expected to see them in one form, and they appeared to you in an entirely new way.

Jesus appears to Mary, but she does not see him at first. In her grief she holds powerful assumptions about what has happened. She grasps onto an image of her beloved friend, which no longer matches the reality. This encounter is Mary's moment of call, as Jesus sends her to witness to the disciples. She is being ushered on a new pilgrimage. The trajectory of her life is altered by this moment.

I am captivated by the image of pilgrimage as a metaphor for our human journeying—not just the physical journeys we make to outward places but also the spiritual journeys we make to the interior places of the heart, the new landscapes we are called to explore. Can we allow our own trajectories to be oriented in a new direction? What new directions has this time of reading and retreat opened to you? How have the angels and the dead—whether saint or ancestor—appeared to you in new ways?

Often the call arrives in our own lives unbidden. Something happens that we did not expect, and we need to shift our perspective to open our eyes to this new possibility. Sometimes it is an unwelcome event such as a death or illness. Sometimes we seek out a new adventure in our lives. Either way, a threshold is a liminal space, meaning a space in between places of security and knowing. On the threshold we are called to release what we thought we knew and our desire to control what is to come. It is an incredibly vulnerable place to be.

Jesus tells Mary, "Do not hold onto me" (Jn 20:17). Do not grasp at this new wonder. Approach with open palms. Be ready to receive the gifts being offered. Know your life direction may take you somewhere unexpected.

I am reminded of one of my favorite stories of the Irish saints. It is said that St. Kevin prayed with arms outstretched and palms open each day. One morning, a blackbird landed in his palm, built a nest, and laid its egg there. Rather than grasping or withdrawing his hand, he held it up for the weeks it took for this new life to be hatched. He received the gift offered to him no matter how uncomfortable. He said yes to what arrived into his life unbidden.

RESURRECTED LIFE

The call of the Christian faith and the resurrection at the heart of its story is this simple invitation: to step forth across the threshold, to release all we thought we knew, to hold our palms open, to say yes to what comes, and then love the world and its inhabitants with all our heart, mind, and soul. The angels, saints, and ancestors are cheering us on. They want us to know the resurrected life here and now. They share their love freely to sustain and inspire us.

Do not hold too tightly to what you think the outcome should be. Let yourself be surprised. Release your expectations and be turned inside out. It is in the places of profound unknowing that we let ourselves enter into mystery. The resurrected life is at heart a great and mysterious process. It is not something we can understand in logical terms; it is only something we can live into and experience.

The heart of this journey has been about attuning ourselves in various ways to the presence of the invisible. By cultivating practices of intuitive knowing, of listening to dreams, of honoring synchronicities, of body sensations, and of simply reaching out in loving care and attention, we have been deepening into intimacy with these holy ones. It is also about finding love in our friendships and connections with one another and trusting those connections endure even beyond the veil.

Henri Nouwen reminds us, "You have to trust that every friendship has no end, that a communion of saints exists among all those, living and dead, who have truly loved God and one another. You know from experience how real this is. Those you have loved deeply and who have died live on in you, not just as memories but as real presences."[1]

How do we find resurrection when there are signs of death all around us through pandemics, wars, gun violence, climate change, and more?

How do we practice a deep sense of hope during so much uncertainty?

What might happen if we let the angels, saints, and ancestors teach us a new way of being?

Imagine if we each took on practices such as these:

- Allow time and space each day to grieve fully, to release the river of tears we try to hold back so carefully.
- Make a commitment to move slowly through the world, resisting the demand for speed and productivity that is tearing our bodies apart and wearing them down to exhaustion. Gift ourselves with rest on behalf of those who could not rest adequately themselves.
- Reject compulsive "busyness" as a badge of pride and see it for what it is: a way of staying asleep to our own deep longings and those of the world around us. Allow time to be present to birdsong and to notice the way creation is awakening through green leaf and pink bud.
- Pause regularly. Breathe deeply. Reject multitasking. Savor one thing in this moment right now. Discover a portal into joy and delight in our bodies through fragrance, texture, shimmering light, song, or sweetness.
- Roll around on the grass, the way dogs do with abandon. Release worries about getting muddy or cold or looking foolish. Or dance with a tree in the wind, letting its branches guide you. Don't hold back.
- Every day, at least once, say thank you for the gift of being alive. Every day, at least once, remember the One who crafted us and all of creation and exclaimed in Genesis, "That is so very good." Each day call upon the angels, saints, and ancestors for wisdom and guidance.

Resurrection calls us into a season of new life and new way of being, which does not mean we deny the reality of death. Indeed, nature requires the death of old matter to generate nourishment for growth. Make space for the sorrow, and make space to listen for the rumblings of new life erupting around you. Let the angels, saints, and ancestors guide you in the practice of celebrating life as it emerges.

THE LOVE OF THOUSANDS

We return to the quote from Linda Hogan that opens this book. Think of all of the love songs, movies about love, poems about love, romance novels, paintings of love, and other expressions of what love is. In many ways, love is the primal force behind what we do and how we live. We create art to understand more deeply what it means to be human. Part of what makes life worth living is our passion, our desire to be in relationship with ourselves, with our beloveds, and with the Divine. Why else would we take the terrible risk of stepping out into the world, revealing our vulnerabilities? What other force is able to compel us to speak our truth?

To be a lover in the world means to be aligned with what sparks our aliveness and passion to help bring healing and wholeness to ourselves and others, to cocreate a more beautiful world with God. Lovers have a healthy sense of embodiment and savor the delights of having a body and senses without shame. They relish the sense experiences of life—the taste of a beautiful meal, the soft fur of a devoted pet, the shimmering of sunlight on water, the music of birds, and the fragrance of jasmine. They uplift the dignity of others, seeing those who are most vulnerable as worthy of love. To abide in love is to celebrate beauty and to know that all of life is a work of art.

When we open our hearts to the blessings of the angels, saints, and our ancestors, we open a river of love. When we heal the wounded in our ancestral line, we remove the blocks and allow love to flow freely.

One of my favorite books is called *Exquisite Desire*, which is about that glorious love poem that appears in the heart of the Hebrew scriptures—the Song of Songs. It is an unabashedly sensual exploration and celebration of erotic love, of the deep desire we have for another person. *Eros* is what draws us out of ourselves and into the world. Through eros we are seduced into a passionate relationship with life.

Rabbi Akiva, who lived in the first century BCE, said that the whole of Torah is holy, but the Song of Songs is the Holy of Holies.[2]

In medieval times, the Song of Songs became the exemplary image of the mystical union between person and Beloved. The language of longing was considered to be the perfect way to express how deep our own longing for God can be and, conversely, how much God longs for and desires us.

When we abide in love we can experience a sense of union with all there is. It is the source of spirituality, especially the mystical paths found in all religious traditions, a sense of the ultimate oneness of everything that is and seeking to experience that unity in daily life. Love calls us into connection with the world. In times when feeling disconnection and isolation is easier than ever, love calls us to step into flesh and blood relationships, to engage, to risk, and to be vulnerable.

Kaitlin Curtice, in her book *Native*, writes, "This is why, when I burn sage or lay tobacco down, I know that I am tethered to a love that has remained steady throughout the centuries and that always calls me back to its own sacredness. And that sacredness will always lead me back out to the world to do the work of love."[3] The practices that tie us to our ancestors both of blood and bone and of spirit keep us tethered to a cord of love that runs through the generations leading to us, calling us to bring more love into the world.

Love is a source of joy, but it also leads to pain. When we love deeply, loss can be wrenching. When we love others, we experience their places of wounding. When they hurt, we hurt as well. Love calls us to be present to the full range of our emotional landscape.

Spiritual writer Joyce Rupp, in her book *Fragments of Your Ancient Name*, writes, "A long ancestral line of women and men proceed ahead of us on our journey, leaving vivid traces of their history. They mark the path with their wisdom, fill the air with fragrant goodness and smile with jubilant satisfaction. You are at the head of this long line with innumerable people of good will. Your light spreads throughout all of them, a great love flowing from them to us."[4]

"A great love flowing from them to us." How you spend your precious moments and what you allow to fill your heart is the call of our pilgrimage of resurrection, to always journey toward love and allow love to flow through you into the world. Pause for a moment to consider this question: What are you in love with? Really passionate, head over heels, and giddy with desire in love with? Have you let love seize your imagination and take hold of you in an absolute way so that your day is spent contemplating ways to spend more time with your Beloved?

One of the great gifts for me personally that has come from doing this work and opening to these presences available to all of us is a deepened sense of community over time. The angels, saints, and ancestors are all cheering us on, sending us love and more love, and asking us to spread it far and wide, to not hold back.

In his book *Confessions of a Funeral Director*, Caleb Wilde writes, "There are literal pieces of your loved ones in you from generations ago. And there will be pieces of your love for generations to come that play out in joy, confidence, and bravery. Love may not be the same as power, and it may not always lead to survival, but love, unlike anything, finds a way to live on."[5] Love is worth cultivating because it endures.

PRACTICE
Surrendering to Love

Angels are beings of light. They surround us with love's protection. Saints are the holy ones who have embraced love as their path and witness to how we too can follow them. Ancestors are both those wise and well ones who have stepped fully into love and also those still-wounded ones aching for the healing that love brings. They remind us of our own humanity. They reveal stories of who we truly are, the longings that beat in our blood.

Sometimes when life feels lonely or challenging in other ways, it can be hard to remember the love of thousands that shimmers just behind the veil between worlds. These beings show us what it means to live so fully that even after death, your love shines through. Continue to build your altar, either one each for the angels, saints, and ancestors, or a larger altar that includes them all together. Keep spending time opening your heart to conversations with them. Continue to pay attention to how they speak to you through your dreams, through your dancing, and through nature's generous speech.

Make time each day to practice softening toward love. Notice the places of holding and tightness in your body, your mind, and your heart, and breathe gently into these places, welcoming love in.

Sometimes we build walls inside ourselves against receiving the fullness of love. Spend some time in reflection to inquire where you find these walls within, always approaching yourself with compassion and grace.

A simple breath prayer can help to soften the walls we have so carefully constructed:

> *Breathe in*: I soften my barriers
> *Breathe out*: to love's abundance.

We may find ourselves yielding to love, savoring love, basking in love, and wanting to share this generous love with others.

The angels, saints, and ancestors, and the love of those thousands, are already awaiting us. We need to simply turn our attention and gaze toward them.

MEDITATION
Experiencing the Love of Thousands

Slow down your breath and gently arrive fully to your body. Notice if your body needs anything for more ease right now. Let your breath guide your awareness from your head to your heart. Enter into this inner sanctuary space, and feel yourself in the presence of the Holy One, whose flame dwells with you always. Offer a moment of gratitude for this deep knowing and connection to the source of all that is.

Pause for a moment and reflect on this journey you have made through this holy season of your life and all of the beings you have deepened your connection and intimacy with.

Call in the presence first of the archangels Michael, Gabriel, Uriel, and Raphael to bring their light of protection, communication, wisdom, and healing to your life right now. Ask your guardian angel to surround you with care. Ask them what they would like you to carry forth from this experience of reflecting on this book. Listen for their response.

Invite in the presence of the Communion of Saints—human, animal, and mineral—to be with you as well and feel the radiance of their love. Notice the energy of the space you inhabit. Call forth your patron saint, the companion who is spending this season with you in special guidance. Ask all of the saints to shower you with their wisdom for this next season of your life and make space for what they want to offer to you.

Invite in all of the wise and well ancestors to surround you, both known to you and the thousands of unknown ancestors who loved, laughed, struggled, grieved, raged, danced, and endured so you could be here. Feel their strength and resilience surrounding you and flowing through your blood and bone. Know this gift in your body as much as possible. Ask them what they want you to know as you continue onward.

Surrounded by this gathering of luminous beings, make a promise to them about how you will continue to show up and honor their presence and love in your life. Name the practices and rituals that you will make time and space for to enrich these relationships.

See them all raising their hands in blessing and showering golden light all around you.

Suddenly a piece of music begins playing, and everyone feels the urge to dance. It might be a slow dance or a fast one as you feel moved to respond. You see the winged angels dancing with the haloed saints and the ancestors in one giant celebration of love.

The crowd separates as a long table piled high with delicious foods and drinks from all the cultures of your ancestors is brought forth. There is more than enough for everyone, and you feast and you dance together for a long while.

Eventually you feel a beautiful sense of fullness, a sense of having enough and knowing there is still an abundance. You know you can call forth this holy dance party any time you need to remember the love of thousands showering down upon you.

You smile as you make way to depart while they continue to laugh and sing. They are waving to you now and reminding you to come back very soon.

You deepen your breath and slowly return to your physical body and the room you are in. Spend some time with a journal, writing down anything you want to remember.

CREATIVE EXPLORATION
Celebrating You

That they would all be joined
together in this moment,
his ancestors and mine cheering us
on as our lips met for the first time,
how his kiss taught me what words
could never, that grief does not last forever,
that the loving gaze of another is enough
to wake us up to the truth about ourselves,
and even now after thousands more kisses,
after learning that pleasure is so sweet,
never to be resisted, how the elders
know this and from behind the veil
love me for saying yes.[6]

For this closing creative exploration, I invite you to reflect on something significant in your life. It could be an intimate partnership, a deep and abiding friendship, a sense of purpose in your life, work that brings you fulfillment and joy, or a commitment to the well-being of others. If you are in an especially difficult time of your life and nothing comes to mind, consider focusing on perseverance and endurance through the challenges of living in this world.

Spend some time deciding on the focus, and then imagine the angels, saints, and ancestors cheering you on and celebrating you. You could choose just one of these groups of invisible beings or all three. In the sample poem I shared above, I wanted to celebrate how the ancestors would have loved my partnering with my husband.

Then do some freewriting, imagining their joy for you. Describe it in as much detail as you can. Write a poem of praise and gratitude.

Blessings as you go forward, bringing love to all the corners of the world.

A Blessing of the Love of Thousands

May the Beloved,
whose delight is imprinted on every cell,
let love seize us, shake us, awaken us
to a new world and way of being.
Let this joy open your palms
to say yes to what comes,
to love the world
with all your heart, mind, and soul.
This blessing lifts the veil between worlds,
and attunes you to the presence of the invisible,
so you see the angels, saints, and ancestors
showering their love freely to sustain and inspire you.
May you receive their love notes
in dreams, synchronicities, intuition,
the knowing of the body and heart.
May they reveal the jewels hidden in the wounds
when love opens our tender places.
May they help you remember
you are never alone, but always breathing
with a multitude, a throng of lovers.
Feel their primal force
tethering you to the cord of love
running through generations,
binding you in union to all there is,

all there ever was,
and all that is yet to come.

ACKNOWLEDGMENTS

As always, I am deeply grateful to my husband, John, who has supported me wholeheartedly these last thirty-plus years in all my creative dreamings. Our move to Europe in 2012 was to follow an ancestral call, and our shared adventure has been a profound gift.

I also extend great thanks to my spiritual director, Dr. Terrill Gibson, who welcomed me into his office almost twenty years ago after my mother died and set me on the path of ancestral healing work. He continues to be a treasured *anam cara* in my life, and I am grateful for his wisdom and the power of Zoom to continue relationships despite overseas moves.

I know well that the travels I have been able to engage in are a great privilege of my life that I never take for granted. I honor all the lands where the bones of my ancestors are buried and how each pilgrimage has helped me to feel a bit more sense of belonging on this beautiful earth.

I have offered this material in various formats over the years, and the wonderful response from participants has kept me going in confidence that there is something worthwhile here to explore. Teaching is such a fertile ground for writing, and I learn as much from my students as I am able to offer them. I am grateful to the Collegeville Institute for allowing me to participate in an online summer program led by Dori Baker and Patrice Gopo. Many of the readings and conversations there worked their way into my ideas.

It is a great joy to continue working with Ave Maria Press, especially my editor for my last several books, Amber Elder. Amber and the whole publishing team continue to celebrate my writing, and I deeply appreciate the ease and shared vision of our working together.

NOTES

1. Calling on the Archangels

1. Peter Stanford, *Angels: A History* (London: Hodder & Stoughton, 2020), 154.

2. Stanford, *Angels*, 9.

3. We will explore the guardian angels in Chapter 2.

4. Stanford, *Angels*, 174.

5. David Albert Jones, *Angels: A Very Short Introduction* (Oxford: Oxford University Press, 2011), 53.

6. Rachel Barenblat, "Bedtime Angels," *Velveteen Rabbi* (blog), July 16, 2015, https://velveteenrabbi.blogs.com/blog/2015/07/bedtime-angels.html.

7. See Rabbi David A. Cooper's *The Handbook of Jewish Meditation Practices: A Guide for Enriching the Sabbath and Other Days of Your Life* (Woodstock, VT: Jewish Lights, 2000), 148–50, for another version of this meditation with slightly different associations.

2. Encountering Your Guardian Angel

1. Origen, *De Principiis* (London: CreateSpace Independent Publishing, 2016), 2, 10, 7.

2. Jean Danielou, *The Angels and Their Mission: According to the Fathers of the Church* (Pine Beach, NJ: The Newman Press, 1957), 68.

195

3. Thomas Aquinas, *Summa Theologica* (Claremont, CA: Coyote Canyon Press, 2010), I, Q. 113.

4. Danielou, *Angels and Their Mission*, 73.

5. bell hooks, *All About Love: New Visions* (New York: William Morrow, 2001), 225–27.

6. hooks, *All About Love*, 234.

7. For more about the practice of breath prayer, see *Breath Prayer: An Ancient Practice for the Everyday Sacred* by Christine Valters Paintner (Minneapolis, MN: Broadleaf Books, 2021).

8. Gregory, *Moralia in Job* (Collegeville, MN: Liturgical Press, 2014). (Quoted in Stanford, *Angels*, 165.)

9. Peter Stanford, *Angels: A History* (London: Hodder & Stoughton, 2020), 157–158.

10. Teresa of Avila, *The Life of St. Teresa of Avila* (New York: Penguin, 1988), 209.

11. Quoted in Stanford, *Angels*, 160.

12. Benedict, *St. Benedict's Rule*, trans. Judith Sutera (Collegeville, MN: Liturgical Press, 2021), 51–52.

13. Hildegard of Bingen, *Scivias*, trans. Columba Hart and Jane Bishop (New York: Paulist Press, 1990), 139.

14. Hildegard, *Scivias*, 143.

15. Hildegard of Bingen, *Symphonia*, trans. Barbara Newman (Ithaca, NY: Cornell University Press, 1988), 20.

16. Luci Shaw, "Angels Everywhere," in *Angels Everywhere: Poems* (Brewster, MA: Paraclete Press, 2022), 11. Used by permission of Paraclete Press, www.paracletepress.com.

3. WRESTLING WITH ANGELS

1. Charles Wesley, "Wrestling Jacob," All Poetry, accessed January 31, 2023, https://allpoetry.com/Wrestling-Jacob.

2. Mary Oliver, "Angels," found at *Writer in the Pines* (blog) by seasweetie, February, 11, 2021, https://writerinthepines.wordpress.com/2021/02/11/angels-by-mary-oliver/.

3. Michael Abramsky, "Jacob Wrestles the Angel: A Study in Psychoanalytic Midrash," *International Journal of Transpersonal Studies* 29, no. 1 (2010): 113.

4. Rainer Maria Rilke, "Der Schauende," in *Book of Images*, original German version on this web page: www.rilke.de/gedichte/der_schauende.htm, (unpublished translation by Christine Valters Paintner and Katharina Resch).

5. Benedicta Ward, trans., *The Sayings of the Desert Fathers: The Alphabetical Collection* (Collegeville, MN: Liturgical Press, 1984), 83.

6. Ward, *Sayings of the Desert Fathers*, 139.

7. Ward, *Sayings of the Desert Fathers*, 231.

4. We Are All Called to Be Saints and Mystics

1. Kenneth L. Woodward, "'Lived from the Heart': An Interview with Bernard McGinn, Part One," *Catholic Outlook*, January 27, 2022, https://catholicoutlook.org/lived-from-the-heart-an-interview-with-bernard-mcginn/.

2. Woodward, "'Lived from the Heart.'"

3. Thomas Merton, *New Seeds of Contemplation* (New York: New Directions Books, 1961), 31–32.

4. Merton, *New Seeds of Contemplation*, 30–31.

5. Embodied Love

1. Peter Brown, *The Cult of the Saints: Its Rise and Function in Latin Christianity* (Chicago: University of Chicago Press, 2014), 1.

2. Brown, *Cult of the Saints*, 3.

3. Brown, *Cult of the Saints*, 4.

4. Brown, *Cult of the Saints*, 9.

5. Brown, *Cult of the Saints*, 75.

6. Brown, *Cult of the Saints*, 50.

7. Brown, *Cult of the Saints*, 58.

8. Christine Valters Paintner, "St. Hildegard Gives Her Writing Advice," in *The Wisdom of Wild Grace: Poems* (Brewster, MA: Paraclete Press, 2020), 20–21. Copyright 2020 by Christine Valters Paintner. Used by permission of Paraclete Press, www.paracletepress.com.

6. Saints and Pilgrimage

1. Hildegard of Bingen, *The Book of Divine Works*, trans. Nathaniel M. Campbell (Washington, D.C.: Catholic University of America Press, 2018), 33–34.

7. Blessings of Our Ancestors

1. Principles excerpted and adapted from Daniel Foor, *Ancestral Medicine: Rituals for Personal and Family Healing* (Rochester, VT: Inner Traditions/Bear & Company, 2017), 22, Kindle.

2. In this book, I draw upon the work of different streams of teaching, including Jungian thought, family systems theory, epigenetics, Christian and Jewish traditions, and teachings from modern thinkers, who have created a whole system of ways to engage with those who have gone before us that are not particular to one religious tradition.

3. Sandra Easter, *Jung and the Ancestors: Beyond Biography, Mending the Ancestral Web* (London: Muswell Hill Press, 2016), Kindle.

4. Cole Arthur Riley, *This Here Flesh: Spirituality, Liberation, and the Stories That Make Us* (New York: Convergent Books, 2022), 60.

5. Patrick B. Reyes, *The Purpose Gap: Empowering Communities of Color to Find Meaning and Thrive* (Louisville, KY: Westminster John Knox Press, 2021), 156.

6. Reyes, *Purpose Gap*, 164.

7. Barbara A. Holmes, *Joy Unspeakable: Contemplative Practices of the Black Church* (Minneapolis, MN: Fortress Press, 2017), 59.

8. Vincent Harding, "I Hear Them . . . Calling," in *Callings*, ed. James Y. Holloway and Will D. Campbell (New York: Paulist Press, 1974), 38–39.

9. Harding, "I Hear Them," 39.

10. "Office for the Dead," Divine Office, accessed December 29, 2022, https://divineoffice.org/office-for-the-dead.

11. Caleb Wilde, *All the Ways Our Dead Still Speak: A Funeral Director on Life, Death, and the Hereafter* (Minneapolis, MN: Broadleaf Books, 2022), 162.

12. Malidoma Patrice Somé, *The Healing Wisdom of Africa: Finding Life Purpose through Nature, Ritual, and Community* (New York: TarcherPerigee, 1999), 53.

13. Gary Eberle, *Sacred Time and the Search for Meaning* (Boston: Shambhala Publications, 2002), loc. 2657–61, Kindle.

14. Henri J. M. Nouwen, *Bread for the Journey: A Daybook of Wisdom and Faith* (San Francisco: HarperOne, 1997), entry for August 29.

15. See the Somatic Experiencing International website at https://traumahealing.org.

16. Ann Patrick Ware, "A Geneology of Jesus Christ," in *Remembering the Women: Women's Stories from Scripture for Sundays and Festivals*, ed. J. Frank Henderson (Chicago: Liturgy Training Publications, 1999), viii. You can find the genealogy reprinted online from JoMae Spoelhof, "Remembering the Women," Medium, December 12, 2021, https://jomae.medium.com/remembering-the-women-92510a4d0f7b.

17. Easter, *Jung and the Ancestors*.

8. Intergenerational Wounds and Our Responsibilities

1. Since those early days sitting in my analyst's office, there has been much more written about ancestral lineage healing from different perspectives. In more recent years, I have found several books helpful, such as Rabbi Tirzah Firestone's *Wounds into Wisdom: Healing Intergenerational Jewish Trauma*, Mark Wolyn's *It Didn't Begin with You: How Inherited Family Trauma Shapes Who We Are and How to End the Cycle*, and Sandra Easter's *Jung and the Ancestors: Beyond Biography, Mending the Ancestral Web*.

2. Malidoma Patrice Somé, *Of Water and the Spirit: Ritual, Magic, and Initiation in the Life of an African Shaman* (New York: TarcherPerigee, 1995), 10.

3. James Baldwin, *Notes of a Native Son* (Boston: Beacon Press, 2014), Kindle.

4. Michael Meade, *Fate and Destiny: The Two Agreements of the Soul* (Housatanic, MA: GreenFire Press, 2012).

5. Toko-pa Turner, *Belonging: Remembering Ourselves Home* (Salt Spring Island, BC: Her Own Room Press, 2018), 148.

6. Turner, *Belonging*, 152.

7. Barbara Holmes, *Joy Unspeakable: Contemplative Practices of the Black Church* (Minneapolis, MN: Fortress Press, 2017), 58.

8. Daniel Foor, *Ancestral Medicine: Rituals for Personal and Family Healing* (Rochester, VT: Bear and Company, 2017).

9. Carl Jung, *Memories, Dreams, Reflections* (New York: Vintage Books, 1989), 401–2.

10. Jenny Brown and Lauren Errington, eds., *Bowen Family Systems Theory in Christian Ministry: Grappling with Theory and Its Application through a Biblical Lens* (Neutral Bay, Australia: Family Systems Practice and Institute, 2019), 29, Kindle.

11. Krista Tippett, "Rachel Yehuda: How Trauma and Resilience Cross Generations," *On Being*, November 9, 2017, https://onbeing.org/programs/rachel-yehuda-how-trauma-and-resilience-cross-generations-nov2017.

12. Jung, *Memories*, 233.

13. Mark Wolynn, *It Didn't Start with You: How Inherited Family Trauma Shapes Who We Are and How to End the Cycle* (New York: Penguin, 2017), 1, Kindle.

14. Thich Nhat Hanh, *The Art of Communicating* (San Francisco: HarperOne, 2014), 151–52.

15. Joy Mannen, *Family Constellations: A Practical Guide to Uncovering the Origins of Family Conflict* (Berkeley, CA: North Atlantic Books, 2009), 33–34.

16. Mannen, *Family Constellations*, 33–34.

17. C. G. Jung, "The Psychological Foundations of Belief in Spirits," in *The Collected Works of C. G. Jung, vol. 8, Structure and Dynamics of the Psyche*, ed. and trans. Gerhard Adler and R. F. C. Hull, 301–18 (Princeton, NJ: Princeton University Press, 2014), 315.

18. Wolynn, *It Didn't Start with You*, 2, Kindle.

19. Wolynn, *It Didn't Start with You*, 61.

20. Wolynn, *It Didn't Start with You*, 63.

21. Turner, *Belonging*, 152.

22. Tirzah Firestone, *Wounds into Wisdom: Healing Intergenerational Jewish Trauma* (Rhinebeck, NY: Monkfish Book Publishing, 2019), 7.

9. Grieving Our Losses

1. I learned of her while reading Christena Cleveland's wonderful book *God Is a Black Woman* (San Francisco: HarperOne, 2022).

2. Holmes, *Joy Unspeakable*, 85.

3. Makoto Fujimura, *Art + Faith: A Theology of Making* (New Haven, CT: Yale University Press, 2021), 121.

4. Walter Brueggemann, *The Prophetic Imagination* (Minneapolis, MN: Fortress Press, 2018), 11.

5. Brueggemann, *Prophetic Imagination*, 3.

10. Ancestral Pilgrimage

1. Phil Cousineau, *The Art of Pilgrimage: The Seeker's Guide to Making Travel Sacred* (Coral Gables, FL: Conari Press, 2012), xxix.

2. Victor Turner, *Dramas, Fields, and Metaphors: Symbolic Action in Human Society* (Ithaca, NY: Cornell University, 1974), 197.

3. Toko-Pa Turner, *Belonging*, 236.

4. Easter, *Jung and the Ancestors*.

5. Kaitlin Curtice, *Native: Identity, Belonging, and Rediscovering God* (Grand Rapids, MI: Brazos Press, 2020), xiv.

6. Christine Valters Paintner, "I Come from People," in *Love Holds You: Poems and Devotions for Times of Uncertainty* (Brewster, MA: Iron Pen, 2023), 126. Used by permission of Paraclete Press, www.paracletepress.com.

11. Cosmology, Myth, and Song

1. I am grateful for the online program I participated in called Singing the Bones from School for the Great Turning which pointed me to many helpful resources for finding myths and songs from my ancestors (https://schoolforthegreatturning.com/).

2. Lyla June, "Reclaiming Our Indigenous European Roots," *MOON Magazine*, January 27, 2019, https://moonmagazineeditor. medium.com/lyla-june-reclaiming-our-indigenous-european-roots-64685c7fc960.

3. Randy Woodley, *Becoming Rooted: One Hundred Days of Reconnecting with Sacred Earth* (Minneapolis, MN: Broadleaf Books, 2022), 164–65.

4. Elie Wiesel, *Night*, trans. Marion Wiesel (New York: Hill and Wang, 2006), xii.

12. BECOMING A WISE AND WELL ANCESTOR

1. Alice Walker, *In Search of Our Mothers' Gardens: Womanist Prose* (Orlando, FL: Harvest Book, 1983), 240.

2. Clarissa Pinkola Estés, *Untie the Strong Woman: Blessed Mother's Immaculate Love for the Wild Soul* (Boulder, CO: Sounds True, 2013), 53.

3. Rowen White, "Nourishing," in *What Kind of Ancestor Do You Want to Be?* ed. John Hausdoerffer et al. (Chicago: University of Chicago Press, 2021), 225.

4. Stephen Lewis, Matthew Wesley Williams, and Dori Baker, *Another Way: Living and Leading Change on Purpose* (Saint Louis, MO: Chalice Press, 2020), 101–2.

5. Reyes, *Purpose Gap*, 12.

6. Winona LaDuke, "How to Be Better Ancestors," in Hausdoerffer et al., *What Kind of Ancestor Do You Want to Be?* 143.

7. Woodley, *Becoming Rooted*, 1–2.

8. Leny Mendoza Strobel and Kamea Chayne, "Leny Mendoza Strobel: Finding Belonging and Remembering How to Dwell in Place," August 10, 2021, in *Green Dreamer*, podcast, episode 320, https://greendreamer.com/podcast/dr-leny-strobel-center-for-babaylan-studies.

9. You can learn more about InterPlay on the website interplay.org.

13. ANCESTRAL EARTH AND DEEP TIME

1. Sharon Blackie, *If Women Rose Rooted: A Life-Changing Journey into Authenticity and Belonging* (Tewkesbury, UK: September Publishing, 2016), Kindle.

2. Katherine Kassouf Cummings, "Moving with the Rhythms of Life," in Hausdoerffer et al., *What Kind of Ancestor Do You Want to Be?* 90.

3. Merton, *New Seeds of Contemplation*, 31.

4. Marcia Bjornerud, *Timefulness: How Thinking Like a Geologist Can Help Save the World* (Princeton, NJ: Princeton University Press, 2018), 16.

5. Thomas Berry, *The Great Work: Our Way into the Future* (New York: Bell Tower, 2000), 161.

6. Berry, *Great Work*, 160.

7. Berry, *Great Work*, 162

8. Karel Schrijver and Iris Schrijver, *Living with the Stars: How the Human Body is Connected to the Life Cycles of the Earth, the Planets, and the Stars* (Oxford: Oxford University Press, 2015), 1, Kindle.

9. Schrijver and Schrijver, *Living with the Stars*, 8–9.

10. Sophie Strand, "Your Body Is an Ancestor," *Braided Way*, November 16, 2021, https://braidedway.org/your-body-is-an-ancestor.

11. Christine Valters Paintner, *Earth, Our Original Monastery: Cultivating Wonder and Gratitude through Intimacy with Nature* (Notre Dame, IN: Sorin Books, 2020).

12. Jung, *Memories*, 233.

Conclusion

1. Henri Nouwen, *The Inner Voice of Love: A Journey through Anguish to Freedom* (New York: Doubleday, 1996), 81.

2. Jonathan Kaplan, "The Holy of Holies or the Holiest? Rabbi Akiva's Characterization of Song of Songs in Mishnah Yadayim 3:5," in *"It's Better to Hear the Rebuke of the Wise than the Song of Fools" (Qoh 7:5): Proceedings of the Midrash Section*, Society of Biblical Literature, vol. 6, ed. W. David Nelson and Rivka Ulmer, Judaism in Context 18 (Piscataway, NJ: Gorgias Press, 2015), 63.

3. Curtice, *Native*, 72.

4. Joyce Rupp, *Fragments of Your Ancient Name: 365 Glimpses of the Divine for Daily Meditation* (Notre Dame, IN: Sorin Books, 2001), November 1.

5. Caleb Wilde, *Confessions of a Funeral Director: How the Business of Death Saved My Life* (New York: HarperCollins, 2017), 136.

6. Christine Valters Paintner, "First Kiss," in *Love Holds You: Poems and Devotions for Times of Uncertainty* (Brewster, MA: Iron Pen, 2023), 124. Used by permission of Paraclete Press, www.paracletepress.com.

Christine Valters Paintner is the online abbess for Abbey of the Arts, a virtual monastery offering classes and resources on contemplative practice and creative expression. She earned a doctorate in Christian spirituality from the Graduate Theological Union in Berkeley, California, and achieved professional status as a registered expressive arts consultant and educator from the International Expressive Arts Therapy Association. She is also trained as a spiritual director and supervisor.

Paintner is the author of seventeen books on monasticism and creativity, including *Sacred Time*; *Earth, Our Original Monastery*; *The Soul's Slow Ripening*; *Water, Wind, Earth, and Fire*; *The Artist's Rule*; *The Soul of a Pilgrim*; *Illuminating the Way*; *The Wisdom of the Body*; and three collections of poetry. She is a Benedictine oblate living in Galway, Ireland, with her husband, John. Together they lead online retreats at their website AbbeyoftheArts.com.

abbeyofthearts.com
Facebook: @AbbeyoftheArts
Instagram: @abbeyofthearts
YouTube: @abbeyoftheartsireland

MORE BY
CHRISTINE VALTERS PAINTNER

Birthing the Holy
Wisdom from Mary to Nurture Creativity and Renewal

Earth, Our Original Monastery
Cultivating Wonder and Gratitude through Intimacy with Nature

Eyes of the Heart
Photography as a Christian Contemplative Practice

Illuminating the Way
Embracing the Wisdom of Monks and Mystics

Sacred Time
Embracing an Intentional Way of Life

The Artist's Rule
Nurturing Your Creative Soul with Monastic Wisdom

The Soul of a Pilgrim
Eight Practices for the Journey Within

The Soul's Slow Ripening
12 Celtic Practices for Seeking the Sacred

The Wisdom of the Body
A Contemplative Journey to Wholeness for Women

Water, Wind, Earth, and Fire
The Christian Practice of Praying with the Elements